FLIGHT

FLIGHT

The Dance of Freedom

A Memoir By

Susan Slotnick

Contents

Dedicated to:

the memory of Dave Navarro,
and all my friends now freed, my friends still imprisoned

And special thanks to:

Anne Pyburn Craig
Chris Belluzzi
Jean King
Bethany Noel
Michael Cacchio
My daughters Rebekah Sarah and Elianah
And most importantly
My husband Sam Slotnick

Foreword

Thinking Out Loud: Finding Gratitude

When I called my best friend Steven and told him about the dance class I signed up for while residing at Woodbourne Correctional Facility, it amused him. "You?" he asked, after five minutes of laughter. "Since when have you been interested in stuff like that?"

True—dancing never did cross my mind before my incarceration in 2009, and at thirty-nine years old, I questioned myself. Do I have the patience? Does my body stand a chance? Can I bear the stones some of my incarcerated peers would surely cast first? Despite my hesitation, I took the risk. "One session surely wouldn't hurt," I said to myself. "One, then I could say at least I tried it."

That was more than sixty sessions ago.

I found out that the sweet and diminutive instructor, Susan Slotnick, has taught at the facility for the past nine years. She displays amazing energy and core strength; at the zesty age of sixty-eight, she can make even the fittest students run on fumes. Planks, sit-ups, you name it—the lady is a supercharged Jane Fonda. [See the *Dance Studio Life* "Generous Heart" Awards, July 2014.]

She's also very philosophical. Every movement or position she teaches has profound reasoning behind it. "Before you do anything," she said, addressing the class on the first day, "take a moment to be present." We all stood facing forward, legs shoulder-width apart, arms strongly held to our sides, eyes on whatever was in front of us.

I discovered that if we are still, the stillness has meaning. What am I envisioning? Who am I thinking of? The answers range from sad to happy, depending on what I'm envisioning or who I'm thinking of.

Almost immediately after our warm-ups of roll-downs and flat-backs, Susan began teaching us a routine. The piece, choreographed to the gospel song "Be Grateful," was challenging to us in our current situation. As a person who has caused a tundra of hurt, I have to think—what is it that I'm grateful for? The question is bizarre, but it is important to ponder.

Susan believes she can change the world's perception about incarcerated individuals—not all of us are animals; not all of us are beyond redemption. Recently she expressed those sentiments in a radio documentary produced by David Gutnick for Canadian Broadcasting Corporation Radio. The documentary touched the hearts of many of its listeners, earning the humanitarian based Gabriel Award [sponsored by the Catholic Academy for Communications Arts Professionals] for CBC Radio in 2014. As a veteran director/choreographer, Susan is a professional, but her professionalism is nothing compared to her compassion for the human struggle.

On my own mission of redemption, I'm amazed to have discovered the restorative quality dancing contains. Who knew there was peace within a *plié*? Or tranquility behind a *battement tendu*? I didn't, and now I embrace the art form. It's more to me than a therapeutic tool in my expanding shed of positive development; it is an actual liberating experience. "Think of this as a gateway to temporary freedom," Susan often tells us.

And I do.

My life has been plagued with self-created adversity, which explains why I have always felt incredibly crappy. Dancing changed that. I now love feeling awesome, alive, and invigorated, even if the techniques are strenuous. Sometimes it is a strained hamstring, sometimes it is a kink in my lower back—but I overcome the pain because of my innate desire to better myself.

For six months I have danced in front of large, clear windows inside the classroom we utilize as our studio, but I don't mind the exposure, nor am I intimidated by the few who walk by and mock us. I've learned to block them out. How? By turning up the volume on my dancing. Each step stomps out their bullying words; each move blurs their hateful stares. I am present, and I am centered. I dance for me, and my friend Steven respects that.

There is no doubt in my mind. I know exactly what I'm grateful for.

Edwin Santana
Dance Studio Magazine
November 2014

Chapter 1

Caged Boys Dancing

In the five years of Sundays I spent in the boys' prison, Rivera was only the second boy to tell me of his crime. I never asked any of them.

Rivera stood before me, edgy, resolute. He spoke with urgency as the other students entered the auditorium. "Please, Miss Susan. I've been thinking about this all week. I have to tell you my crime. I raped my four-year-old sister, and now I can never go home because my victim is in the house," Rivera blurted out. "They'll send me to a shelter or an adult prison when I turn eighteen."

I had no absolution to offer, no emotional response, no shock, and no sympathy. All I could or would give was a new way to move. "Take off your shoes," I said. "It's time to dance." Minutes later Rivera was moving tenderly, gracefully, focused upward, slowly raising his arms with the rest of the dancers as the Boys' Choir of Harlem sang "Amazing Grace." At the end of the class he told me the other part: when he got back to his cell he planned to drop his gang flag on the floor. Only years later did I learn that dropping the flag was the final act of renouncing gang affiliation.

The only other boy who'd confided in me said a "rich White girl" had approached him as he was dancing with his crew in the 57th Street subway station, boom box blasting, sweat pouring, hormones radiating.

"She wanted it," he told me, but she'd later told police that he attacked her in a dank dark corner of the subway. She was 14; he was 16. In the eyes of the law he was a sex offender.

The other boys flocked towards me, each one wanting all my energy. They were always desperate for more one-to-one attention before and after class than I could possibly deliver. Many wrote me long letters; I read and responded as best I could. How hungry they all were for the simple presence of one who was not there to judge, punish, or compete.

There was so much I didn't know when I began prison work, but I held fast to the one thing I did know from direct experience: the power of the body to move in beautiful ways. Dancing can wipe away disgrace and humiliation and, in that moment, recapture lost innocence.

I'd learned this at seventeen after getting into a car with Sal Pellegrino, a known bad boy. I'd lied to my parents and met him on the street corner. Our "date" turned out to be degrading; the opposite of what I hoped for—love and romance. He took me to the pool room where he spent time making money as a fledgling pool shark. Afterward, he raped me.

Although today that would be considered a "date rape," in those days the phrase hadn't yet been coined. It never occurred to me to see myself as a victim. I knew I was a loser, flunking every subject in school. Eyes outlined in heavy black, sauntering around in tight clothes, chewing a wad of gum. You remember the girls like me—tough-acting, "slutty" girls, flicking away the butt of cigarette after cigarette with disdainful grace.

Fifty years ago, it was assumed that such girls deserved whatever they got. It wasn't cool to be fazed by rape, any more than it was cool to be fazed by bad grades or my mother's expectations. But the pain gnawed through the layers of my tough-chick persona; both the event and the realization of how badly I was lying to myself about who I was and what I secretly wanted: a happy life filled with self-love. The lack caused deep, private sadness. There was nowhere to turn, no help at hand.

2

After the rape I crept downstairs and danced until morning, until the memory of losing my virginity in such ugliness faded, erased by the last notes of the Drifters singing "Some Kind of Wonderful."

I loved to dance but I did not have the discipline and perseverance to become a dancer. The years that I might have spent training my body to flawless execution had already been squandered. Although I would never be the ballerina I hoped to be, I would always remember the healing I found in dance. As my adult life unfolded, I began to bridge the gap between the rarefied world of dance and my desire to teach dance as a healing art to children and underserved populations.

Teaching small-town school children was rewarding, especially when parents and teachers told me that the students were inspired by what they learned. Working with my own youth dance company, a diverse group of talented kids, was a joy. Still, I yearned to test out my insights about what dance could do in situations where children were physically not free since I knew that dance could allow then to feel free, if only briefly.

The opportunity to teach in the nearby boy's prison came through my daughter's friend's mom, a GED teacher at the facility. She recommended me and got me in the door to be interviewed by the director of volunteer services, who turned out to be a remarkable woman in a pitched battle with the cancer that had already taken one of her eyes. I was given permission to begin the following week.

The gleaming, heavy wire fence seemed to appear out of nowhere. You rounded a bend at the end of a long, dimly lit country road through deep woods and came upon it, an odd and angular thing to encounter out in the Hudson Valley byways. Moonlight glinted on the metal razor wire like a strange huge ornament suspended low in the night sky. My first night there, parked by the prison gate, I'd turned off my car and tried to start it again, just to be certain of a getaway plan. It took several tries to get the ignition to catch, maybe an omen, I thought. It was my first time inside a prison and I was scared.

I showed ID and was buzzed through a heavy door, then led to an auditorium. They arrived, the fifteen boys who'd volunteered to dance; eight African Americans, six Hispanics and one Caucasian. (In the five years I spent working in that facility and in the twelve years I taught in an adult men's prison, that demographic mix remained the same.)

All the boys were dressed in bright red sweat pants and matching t-shirts. I was surprised; I knew red was the signature color for the Bloods street gang, and that colors were outlawed in prison. Red, an officer explained, made it easier to spot a runaway.

They stood before me, fifteen young men. We looked each other over. Here they were, the outcasts, portrayed in their fifteen minutes of name-withheld fame as society's nightmares. They gazed at me with a mix of excitement and suspicion.

Their t-shirts were pressed, their sweat pants hung low on their hips, their hair was combed or braided. Who they had been at the instant in time they had done whatever they had done, I could not know: in this moment of beginning, and in the many moments we would share, they were just boys.

"Move as if you are swimming at the bottom of the ocean, displacing tons of warm heavy water all around you." Doing so, movement will become smooth, the imagined resistance of the water creating a sense of muscular power and grace. They instantly intuited my meaning, although I found out later that most of them, city kids, had never learned to swim. They danced beautifully from the very first moment they lifted their arms to the swell of music. I hadn't really been certain what kind of beginning to expect, but I hadn't counted on their poignant grace, their utter willingness.

Seeing their talent, I decided to train them exactly as I trained my other students, with pliés, tandus, contractions, flat backs, and com-binations.

4

FLIGHT

They called me "Miss Susan." They were polite and shy with my daughter Elianah and her friend Bethany, who helped with the dance class, the only two girls their own age many had seen in months or years. They did not eat dinner during the allotted break. "I don't eat in front of girls," a boy told me.

Over five years, we staged several full-length concerts. They were allowed to invite their families and I could invite whomever I wanted, and we usually had about 200 people in the audience. On the night of

one performance, a prisoner named Koran handed me a poem which he later recited before the audience:

Dance is a catalyst which fills your soul
The weak become strong and the timid bold
You move in ways that would never be sought
Begin to learn things that could never be taught
If your soul were your son, then dance is your daughter
And without her in your life, you're like a fish out of water
A thought without a brain, a brain without a body
There's a void in your chest without your soul
And only dance will fill the hole
If a picture's worth a thousand words
Then a dance is worth a million
If heaven is perfectness
Dance is what you have until then
The simplest movement like the flick of your wrist
Can deliver a powerful message
Mind and body are the key to dance
But your soul's the actual essence.

The audiences always had questions. That night, it was Koran who answered the one someone always asked.

"How has dancing in prison changed your life?"

"I feel powerful and free," he said. "My self-esteem has skyrocketed. For the first time, I have earned respect. Learning the choreography was the hardest effort I've ever made at anything in my whole life."

The following Sunday, Koran was gone. The boys told me he'd been sent to the adult facility at the county jail with yet another black mark on the record of his young life.

The boys had to ask to be let out of their cells to urinate at night, and a guard, obviously not one worthy of the title "correctional officer," had refused to let Koran out, taunting him, saying, "You'll pee when I tell you."

Koran was still feeling terrific from the high after the performance and the accolades received from his recitation of the poem. Refused permission to fulfill his most basic need, perhaps by a guard who sensed his mood and disliked it, prison crashed in on him with a thud. After repeated, humiliating refusals, when he was finally let out, Koran lost it and punched the officer in the face. Had it been a moment in a movie, the audience would have cheered: in real life, of course, it led him deeper into the system's maw.

Visiting hours at the county jail are jam-packed on weekends. All twenty compartments were occupied most by girlfriends and wives, many towing young children and babies. To be heard, each person had to talk over the people on either side, ratcheting up the decibels to a screaming clamor, amping up the tension and defeating privacy.

Koran was shocked to see me, to have any visitor at all; his family couldn't afford the trip from Harlem. Bits and pieces of surrounding conversations filtered in and out as we talked.

"Did you send me the new shoes I asked for?

"Have you spoken to my brother yet about the money?"

"What's the matter with you? Why haven't you taken the baby to the clinic?"

"Did my lawyer get back to you?"

We were screaming too, yelling at the top of our lungs about Dostoyevsky's *Crime and Punishment*, which Koran was reading. We screeched back and forth about the moral culpability of Rodion Raskolnikov.

"He murdered a dude who was a really bad man to begin with! So what do you think, Susan? Was killing him justified?"

It never occurred to me that boys from gangs might read the classics. One boy often came into the auditorium just before class to play the piano. I was told he was on the "mental case unit" and was failing all of his high school equivalency classes. As soon as he saw me he would stop playing, place his hands in his lap, and stare into space. Once I managed to enter without him seeing me, and listened to him playing a Chopin Prelude he'd picked up by ear without ever having a single lesson.

Prisoners believe that what they learn in secret imprints deeper into their memories. They call it "independent study." It's the difference, they will say, between doing the time and letting the time do you.

As a "misfit" teen in the 7th grade, independent study provided me with a rich secret life. Ellen, a girl in my class, was the object of my admiration. She was Jewish like me, but unlike me she came from a prominent loving family. At the beginning of the day we both came to school well-groomed but by the end of the day I was a dirty ragamuffin and she looked ready for a photo shoot. If I couldn't be like her, at least, I thought, I could read the same book she was reading, *Exodus* by Leon Uris. While I was failing every academic subject, after being inspired by *Exodus*, I devoured everything the White Plains Library about the Holocaust and the Jewish experience in World War II; many thick books. I finished the last book by the time I flunked out of high school six years later. I could recite the names of the concentration camps, what populations were predominant in each, how many people died and what country they came from.

Address Unknown, an obscure book translated from German, consisted of a correspondence between two friends, one Jewish and one German, and ended with the German man's letter returned stamped *Adressat unbekannt*: address unknown. The Jewish man had been taken to a concentration camp. I read scholarly and popular works, but this simple book about the breakdown of a friendship and the death of one man was the most memorable.

I memorized sixty-three poems from *A Shropshire Lad* by Victorian poet A. E. Houseman, poems about dying young, the fleeting nature of love, secret passions, the allure of suicide, and nostalgia for lost youth.

> Into my heart an air that kills
> From yon far country blows,
> What are those blue remembered hills?
> What spires, what farms are those?
> That is the land of lost content,
> I see it shining plain,
> The happy highways where I went and cannot come again.

Chapter 2

How It Happened

There were no happy highways in my memory. My childhood troubles, like many a child's, began before my birth with my parents' marriage. They had known each other for exactly one week. Mother told me that she'd only accepted his proposal because she was twenty-five, an old maid; Dad was financially established, and Mother was extremely materialistic. It was the Great Depression, and a well-off husband was a catch.

My father was an autistic savant with an eidetic memory. He owned a record store. If he handled a record just once he memorized the title, catalog number, and flip-side information, then he put it back on the shelf and remembered where it was among thousands of other records. He committed to memory 250,000 eleven-digit record catalog numbers without effort, but could never recall our ages, what grade we were in, or our birthdays.

Autistic people process information differently and may have a hard time seeing things from a non-autistic perspective. I remember asking my father if I could have a sleepover at a friend's house. I was nine years old and very excited by the possibility, but my father could only relate to how he would experience sleeping away from home.

"No," he said, "You already have a bed here."

When my father was dying, his nurse called me and told me to come as soon as possible. I asked her to ask him if he wanted to see me one more time. "Hold on," she said, I heard her steps going away and a few seconds later returning.

"Your father says he said 'goodbye' to you already." He couldn't relate to my perspective. One goodbye was plenty for him.

Asperger's Syndrome, a disorder on the autism spectrum characterized by significant difficulties in social interaction as well as restricted and repetitive patterns of behavior and interests, was not well understood back then. People living with it were most often just considered "weird." There was no one to help our family understand Dad's behavior or help him understand ours.

My father's store, Merit Music Shop on West 46th Street, was a haven for celebrities of the day like Jimmy Durante, Danny Kaye and Tiny Tim. Dad's specialty was entertaining the customers with his astounding memory.

In this excerpt from the "Only Human" column, in the *New York Daily News*, Tuesday April 14, 1970, it's explained:

> The gentleman asked for the kind of help that made Jack Meltzer glow, 'I want a recording of the song I sang to court my wife. It's for our golden anniversary, I can't remember the name it goes like this'—he hummed it. Jack promptly told him it was 'Sweet September' recorded in 1919 by Al Jolson. Afterward he handed the man the 1923 two-inch-thick Victor catalogue, 'Pick any number.' (There were thousands, like a phone book.) 'What's cl 18921?'
>
> 'That's "Sneak," a foxtrot,' Jack answered. 'The flip side is "Are You Playing Fair," played by the Club Royal Orchestra.'

My father could not read social cues. When I was eight he was invited to perform it on the immensely popular Ernie Kovacs show. I remember my mother turning on the black-and-white TV so that my siblings and I could watch our dad hit the big time. Kovacs blatantly made my father the butt of his jokes, calling him a "leading authority on useless information." People were laughing, the jokes kept coming, but Dad didn't realize he was the brunt of the joke.

Today, I recognize that his awkwardness and memorization skills were textbook symptoms of his particular niche on the spectrum. At eight, I just felt sorry for Dad.

In his store, my father came to life. It was fascinating to observe him in his element, out of Mother's overwhelming shadow. He was talkative and happy among his admiring customers. Some of the most salient aspects of his autistic behavior seemed to dissolve when he talked about music, his greatest love.

Was he autistic? If not for his astounding memorization skills I might have questioned this based on stories from his life BM, Before Mother. He was born in 1902 on Cherry Street, on Manhattan's Lower East Side, at the time considered "the most overcrowded place on earth." According to my father the Lower East Side was both a place where arts and family life flourished and a filthy slum

My father quit school in the 8th grade and went to work to help support the family. There were no indoor toilets, the outhouse his family used was shared with what he remembered as hundreds of other families and had no toilet paper. The children followed food trucks and picked up the beans that often fell to the street. I assume there was no means of birth control, since he had 10 siblings they could not afford to raise. They all slept in the same small tenement room. One bed was for the girls, the other for the boys; they slept sideways with their legs hanging off the bed, five side-by-side boys and five side- by-side girls.

His sister Anna committed the most grievous sin of sins when she ran off with the son of the slumlord who owned the tenement building. He was a gentile! a GOY! It was customary to tear a piece of clothing in mourning as an expression of pain and sorrow. The family did not have clothes that could be sacrificed. Anna was the sacrifice. All 10 children were forbidden to ever see or speak to her again. My father was 16.

And here is the story that surprises me most, since my father was so emotionally removed and detached. He defected and went to see Anna and was kicked out of the house as a result. My father never lied or embellished a story, so when he told me he spend a year as a stevedore on the Mississippi River and witnessed a stabbing, I believed him. I still do.

The first of the siblings to die was my aunt Cora, the youngest. I was 10 years old when we went to her funeral somewhere in the borough of Brooklyn. My mother told me to find my father; she was impatient and wanted to leave at the end of the graveside service. I found him behind a tree crying, his face garishly distorted with pain. I was terrified. My reserved unemotional father was someone who could be overwhelmed, could hurt with power and strength. It struck me afterwards that my father never really bonded with us. His family of origin had used up all his warmth and passion.

In the old days, you didn't need to purchase a record in order to listen. I loved spending entire Saturdays in a small soundproof listening booth at Dad's store. My father taught me how to hold the fragile shiny black vinyl discs by their edges, clean them, and return them to their inner and outer sleeves with loving care.

The toilet in Dad's store held a curious and powerful fascination. It was filthy. At home, the tiniest smudge on any part of a toilet would be instantly wiped clean with much elbow grease and gusto. Dad's toilet represented rebellion, who my father might be if left to his own devices.

Everyone in the family was in secret rebellion against my mother. My brother hid his desire to play with his ventriloquist dummies. My sister spent most of her time alone in her room. I was acting out with boys and men.

In the summer of 1959, I was a fourteen-year-old counselor-in-training at Camp Highmount, and Eddie Leavett was a forty-six-year old Jewish high school teacher from Valley Stream, Long Island.

He told me to sneak out of my cabin at night and hide in his car. We drove away, parked in the woods, and smooched, slobbering like two teenagers.

I wasn't attracted to Mr. Leavett. "Making out" with him was repulsive; it was the power to arouse him and break the camp rules that was the hook. It didn't go any further. If it did I have blocked the memory. I was a willing participant, unaware that I had no legal right to consent, and for the next seven years I received a birthday card signed Humbert Humbert, after the anti-hero of Nabokov's *Lolita*. The last birthday card came on my twenty-first birthday; now that I was an adult, Mr. Leavitt had lost interest. By then, the memory disgusted and shamed me.

In today's world, he might have wound up imprisoned. Sex offenses get murky, running the gamut as they do from violent rape of infants to eighteen-year-old boys having sex with their fourteen-year-old girlfriends.

At twenty-two years old I was almost murdered in Herzliya, Israel by a boy from South Africa. I agreed to take a walk down the deserted beach with him because he was good-looking, well-mannered, and Jewish. Only an hour before the beach had been crowded with families; mothers screaming at their children in crisp guttural Hebrew not to wander too far into the surf. But it was Friday night, the beginning of the Sabbath, and they had all gone home.

I knew it was a risk to go with a stranger, even a Jewish one. But my entire sense of self-worth depended on the one power I could count on: men and boys were attracted to me, and I milked that for whatever drops of attention and self-esteem it provided.

I looked good in my bikini. His eyes were on my body; I saw and pretended not to notice. We'd walked about twenty minutes, maybe a mile down the beach, when a fog rolled in from the sea. Suddenly he had me by my bikini bottom and was pulling me into the water. His nails cut my skin; my hips stung in the salt water.

I got free and began running back up the beach. He was faster; he caught me and knocked me down, trying to yank my bathing suit off. His face had changed. He had a blank, dazed, determined look that scared me.

Time seemed to warp into slow motion. Inwardly, I felt oddly resigned; outwardly, I kept struggling and screaming and running away. He caught me several times, dragging me into the water and trying to push me down. I experienced something I had thought was a myth: my life flashed before my eyes, with it came a strange calm thought that no one would be surprised by how I died.

As abruptly as the attack had begun, it ended. My assailant appeared to come to his senses; the dazed expression gone, he looked tired. We walked together down the beach, back to where I might find help. All the while I was anticipating the next attack.

I ran toward the first people I saw, screaming for help. He ran too, in the other direction. Israeli strangers took me to the police station, where two men in uniforms asked me questions and wrote out a report.

Although I was all scratched up they didn't bother to hide their amusement. "Two tourists, a lovers' quarrel on the beach, we can do nothing! Neither of you are citizens of Israel. Tourists come here and misbehave away from home, we don't get involved."

Apparently, Mother's axiom that any Jew would always help a fellow Jew didn't hold in the Jewish homeland.

I considered all the violations of me partly my fault, the result of bad judgment. If I was partly responsible, I was not a victim, not helpless. And if I did things differently, it wouldn't happen again.

Of course, that's far from the whole truth. Nothing justifies assault or rape. Today it's axiomatic that no means no, but the complete disregard for any and all mitigating circumstances—the woman's drunkenness or poor judgment in choosing who to be alone with, is disempowering to a woman. If a person in the New Year's Eve crowd at Broadway and 42nd Street flashes a hundred-dollar bill and it is grabbed by a stranger, they'll accept that their recklessness contributed to the theft.

It's not that the victim's choices are justifications or mitigating circumstances. A crime is a crime. But protecting oneself is always a good choice.

My first memory of criminal behavior came when I was just nine. My father employed his younger brother Harry, Grandmother Sadie's "favorite," since he was the youngest of her 11, one of whom had died of the flu. Born tiny, he was often sick. The heroine of my father's life, from beginning to end, was his mother, so he carried on taking care of Harry long after my grandmother's death.

I have dusty recollections of Uncle Harry, small and stout with a thick black mustache that covered his upper lip. His sideways half hidden smile seems lascivious and cunning in memory; I could be imagining that, since he turned out to be a criminal.

Money and stock were missing every morning from my father's record store. To catch the thief. police organized a sting operation. They caught the robber in the act by hiding behind stacks of records until the perpetrator entered through an unlocked back door. How my father discovered that Uncle Harry left the door open for the thieves and got his cut of the action, I do not know. I do know that my father never spoke to Harry again, did not attend his funeral, and had no regrets.

That memory helped me make the decision decades later to go "no contact" with my mother. I realized after a lifetime of trying to "fix us" that nothing I could do could stop her jealousy and abuse. Like my father with his brother I did not attend her funeral. I wish I had stopped all contact at 30 instead of 60. That would have saved bundles of hurt on all sides.

I tried at 24 but I could not sustain the estrangement, although I had plenty of provocation. My in-laws had offered to give us the down-payment for a house. My mother-in-law asked my mother for a contribution.

"Your son is a weakling," said my mother. "He sides with Susan when we fight. She doesn't deserve my help." My father would always opt to recede into the wallpaper rather than fight with my mother.

Five decades later, we still live in the house my in-laws provided. Early on we rented a room with a separate entrance and bathroom to help with the costs of homeownership. A few years later my mother announced that she'd be taking over our rental space, bringing in a decorator, and using it as her "northern home" during her visits from Florida. It was an announcement, not a request. Whether my mother remembered refusing to contribute or what she said to my husband's mother about her son I do not know, but one of our early "no contact" periods followed,

I wrote my mother a letter telling her I wanted nothing from her ever again. When my mother died she attached that 30-year-old letter to her will, which left nothing to me, my daughters, or my grandchild.

After my father's store was robbed he became even more removed from the family. It was then, when I was twelve, that I began to notice how much my mother criticized and blamed my father for her intrinsic dissatisfaction.

Dad wasn't Mother's only scapegoat. She routinely acted as though she hated everything about me. Family members have suggested it could have been because of my feisty spirit, which quickly grew into bitter rebellion in the face of her dislike.

My brother Steven's birth was a bright, warm spot in my childhood. I adored Steven and played with him every chance I got. I dressed him up in my Brownie uniform, beanie and all, put him in a red wagon, and carted him around the neighborhood selling Girl Scout cookies. Playing with Steven, I was about as happy as I ever remember being. Mother found it unbearable that we enjoyed each other, and was jealous.

Early on Steven displayed personality traits that alarmed my mother. He cried a lot. He had no idea what to do with a ball, couldn't climb the rope in gym, and had no interest in sports. Children called him homo and sissy. Gender-neutral childrearing was not a concept back then, any more than autism was well understood. Seeing him tormented broke my heart.

The way I chose to express it would change my young life. I borrowed Houseman's rhyming scheme and wrote a poem for English class about seeing him bullied.

I watched him as he played the other day
I heard the others tell him to go away
I understood when he pretended not to hear
He used an old and familiar veneer
But his anguished face, and his pitiful tears
The laughter and name-calling from all of his peers
Brought to my mind a long-past day
When I was the child they told to go away.

My English teacher was amazed to receive the poem from someone who had previously been a big fat zero of a student. Without bothering to mention it to me first, she published it in the school newspaper.

The day that newspaper was distributed started like any typical day. I dressed in my standard, in-your-face "slutty" juvenile-delinquent style. My boyfriend picked me up in his nosed and decked hotrod. We smoked outside the building before first period, which I cut as usual, preferring to spend the morning in the girls' room socializing.

When I emerged from the bathroom reeking of tobacco and hungry for lunch, a popular, "smart" kid rushed over to me, school newspaper in hand.

"Did you write this?"

I glanced down at the printed page to see my own words and managed to admit it, terrified of what would happen next.

"It's very good. I like it a lot."

All day, students congratulated me. By the end of the day, I was lording about the halls soaking up the compliments. For the first time, I toyed with the idea of leaving the hoodlum guise behind. Was it possible to live a life in which my inside self and my outside self matched? Might there be an exit from the miserable prison of self-doubt, fear and shame I'd been living in?

The possibility of a unified, authentic self became what I would pursue all my life.

It was that goal I was chasing when I first heard of the ideas of George Ivanovich Gurdjieff. Gurdjieff was a Russian mystic and spiritual teacher during the early to mid-20th century. He taught that most people live their lives in a state of hypnotic "waking sleep," but that it is possible to transcend that condition and move to a higher state of consciousness, to achieve full human potential and become "real." Gurdjieff developed a method to accomplish this which he called "the work." I practiced the method, "the work," intensively for five years. Authenticity and unification of the self remained my central goal.

Each of us has a private and public self. My quest to have one self began the day my persona and my soul collided when my English teacher outed me.

I later found that the boys in prison understood the idea of a private and public self right away. "Who are you in your cell at night, what do you think about? How is your posture different? What's your predominant emotion when you're alone? Is it the same when you are in the mess hall or the gym?"

I disseminated the "work" practices to the boys, encouraging them to work on staying present, to observe themselves without judgment, to maintain, deepen, and sustain attention. Mastering the choreography was a byproduct of their internal laboratory work: self-observation leading to self-knowledge and on to the ability to move, moment to moment, with awareness of their emotional and physical presence. This was the most important component of the dance program.

From a letter:

> I've been written up, and I was bugging out but yesterday, a kid from another gang was trying to make me mad, so I did the thing we do at the beginning of dance class, watched myself and felt my feet touching the floor like you say, and then I didn't need to sock him anymore. Also, when I saw the boys across the lake swimming, I thought about the dance we are learning, the one about gratitude, about being grateful that I am alive and I was less upset.

The Division for Youth prison in the Mid-Hudson Valley is located on Chodikee Lake, off Route 299 in Highland. The quiet, 100-acre pool of placid water is the jewel of what used to be called the Penn Yan, a desolate, beautiful thickly-forested area that's drawn religious cultists, poets, wild men, farmers, bootleggers, tramps and vacationers over the years. In the springtime, small boats carrying fisherman glide in the water's gentle current; in winter, there are children ice skating.

It was painful for the boys to see the activity on the lake in the summertime, especially when Camp Torah Vodaath, a camp for Hasidic boys their age, was in session. The brown skinned prisoners in their bright red t-shirts and khaki pants were a stark contrast to the pasty-pale Hasidics across the water in their black pants and white shirts, white tzitzis threads dangling at their waists, and skull caps. The Jewish boys spent carefree hours swimming and boating. Sounds of splashing, laughter and happy shouts were heard by the prisoners I had come to love as if they were my own sons. It seemed so unjust that the incarcerated boys could spend years of summers residing on the lake and never put a finger in the cool water.

I know what that felt like. At their age my failing grades required me to attend summer school, confined in a hot, stale classroom all day with no air conditioning. My body felt large, damp, ungainly; heavy make-up melted greasy on my face as I rode home on the school bus past the nearby county pool where the "good kids" frolicked. I did not deserve, had not earned the right, to be in the water with the good kids.

One of the boys said he didn't care. In the hood nobody knew how to swim, and he'd be scared to get into a boat anyway.

One pleasurable activity available to them in the hood, and free, was sex. For every unwed teenage mother there was a father. It never entered my mind that these boys might be teenage fathers, but half of them were.

Letters:

> Hello, my name is Cesar from dance and I am 15 years old. I am here because I caught five charges—robbery, possession of a gun, armed robbery, violation of probation and gang fights. I am a member of the Bloods but I keep that on a low profile. I am about to drop my flag and get out at an early age so I could be there for my children. I have a son named Tyrell, two years old and I have a baby girl named Catalane that is 5 months old and my fiance is also pregnant with a girl that is due this month.

* * *

Dear Miss Susan, I've been jumped by gangs; I never wanted to be myself, so I did what other people wanted. I have been beat up for no reason at all and I have never trusted anyone in my life. I was once an innocent baby but in such a cold world I was guilty of something to the next man. I was brought up by a man who beat my mother all the time; he was always drunk and very violent. I got took from my biological mother who is my heart. I never felt love from anybody until you and Martin [his best friend inside]. Miss Susan, I was once a daddy to a little boy. He was four months old when he died in the hands of a doctor all because my girl didn't want to keep him because he was going to be sick. Before I seen him I felt joy and love until I heard this. I cried for weeks on end. All I wanted was to be a daddy. I am 17 years old and I been through so much pain already...

The night of the last full-scale concert I arrived to find the stage light bulbs were out. I asked the recreation director to change them.

"It's not my job, it's in my union contract. I can't do it. You have to call maintenance."

"Okay, let's get them."

"It's the weekend, they're not here."

Two hundred invited guests, including some of the boy's children, had come to see the show. Family members from New York City were already on the bus headed upstate. I bullied the recreation director into getting on a ladder and fixing the lights. The show went on, but that was curtains for me as far as the Division for Youth was concerned. A dance program was an oddity in the first place. A volunteer telling a staff member what to do was verboten. Shortly after that I was informed the dance program was dropped. It was a terrible blow. I never thought I would have an opportunity to work with incarcerated people again.

I was wrong. For ten years of Sundays now, I have driven over a mountain, through all kinds of weather, to spend time behind the walls with my locked-up dance students. Authorities shook their heads and laughed at first, not believing that adult male prisoners would study modern dance with a middle-aged White woman.

I knew they would. These were the same boys; same demographics, similar histories, separated from their children and loved ones, each moment of their lives a constant reminder of a bad choice. They were just twenty to thirty years older.

Recently my dance company inside of the adult men's facility at Woodbourne Correctional prison performed three choreographed dances for the general population of incarcerated men. The rules are stricter here; there are no invitations for families, and I was limited to inviting only twenty outside guests.

Before all performances we formed a circle and joined hands. To become present, we listened to the sounds around us; the hum of the air vent, the deep voices of the prisoners in the audience, the clanging of a closing gate. We begin our dedication. For whom do these men dance?

"My father who died last year."

"My daughter who just entered college."

"My grandma who raised me."

"All the men who have danced in this program and are now free."

"All the people who love me and want me to come home."

A prisoner named Gavin dedicated his performance to me.

It has seemed mysterious folly to many of my associates, this work of mine inside the walls. Standing in a circle holding hands with them before the performance feels natural, it's where I belong. You'd have to walk in my skin to understand this moment was inevitable.

FLIGHT

I've done a lot of things with my life. I've painted a lot of pictures. I've written a lot of articles. I've probably choreographed over a thousand dances. But somehow, I walk into that room in the prison and get the overwhelming feeling that everything I ever did in my life was a step into that room.

Susan Slotnick

from the introduction to the

film *The Game Changer*

Chapter 3

Nobody Knows Me but Me: Little Susan Meltzer

May 2, 1958

Diary

My mother hates me. I have no friends. I am flunking all my subjects. So why do I believe in myself so much

From my birth on Nov. 11, 1945 in Brooklyn, New York—Armistice Day, a holiday celebrating peace—to the present, I am grateful for every bad and good moment comprising my life.

On the surface, a Westchester County childhood hardly sounds like deprivation, but to the particular child that I was, it was a metaphorical prison—a well-appointed one, but confining all the same.

If it had all been simple, if my parents had been warm and empathetic, if Westchester had been a center of creative ferment and activist politics, I might never have had to develop, by myself, a foundation of self-love and inner strength.

Early on, it was just my older sister Bunny and I at home. My father worked seven days a week; my mother was a compulsive housecleaner, and treated my sister and I as two more objects to be properly maintained and kept spotless.

"Normal" and "presentable" were her top priorities. We were dressed like little models—Brooklyn's own little Jewish Shirley Temple clones, wearing long curls with matching hair ribbons, matching outfits. Every item, from the barrettes in our hair down to the pristine white socks and shoes on our feet, was color-coordinated.

Across the street from our apartment building was a playground where all the stay-at-home mothers, virtually every woman in the 1950's, showed off their children. Mother told me years later while bragging about how fastidious she was that when our white shoes got scuffed during play she would retrieve white shoe polish from her handbag, take us behind a tree and hastily remove the black scars from our shoes. Had she been a man dragging little girls into the bushes, she could have created enough suspicion to be arrested.

When I was five, we moved to Forest Hills, a fashionable location among upwardly mobile Jewish families. Two years later, we built a home in Scarsdale. We were climbing. Mother talked often about how rich and refined our lives would become in Scarsdale.

Our stark pale-grey stone ranch house sat on a quiet corner in a typical suburban Westchester neighborhood. Window shades were always drawn; the only people in the street were white-uniformed, sleep-in "girls" who tended the children and did the housework. To my city-child's eyes, it seemed deserted.

Our "girl" was named Pat. She had dark brown skin and shiny hair, and wore purple lipstick. My mother's relationship with her veered crazily between extremes. When my mother's loneliness got the better of her after a few drinks, Pat was her girlfriend and confidante. At other times, she'd regret these lapses. "I'm letting Pat become too familiar," she'd tell my father. "I need to be more refined, and treat her more like a servant then a friend." One evening, while Pat was serving our dinner, Mother told her it was unseemly for her to wear street clothes. Thereafter she must put on a white uniform, like the other maids in the neighborhood.

I had no such misgivings; I enjoyed Pat's company. She was the sanest adult in the house. When I was nine, she took me to see *Imitation of Life,* one of the earliest Hollywood films dealing with racism. In the movie, the Black family was treated terribly compared to the light-skinned, yellow-haired White family. It made me sad. "I wish you weren't Black," I told Pat as we left the theatre hand in hand.

"Don't ever say that to me again. I'm proud to be Black. I thank God I'm not White."

Those were the first words I ever heard spoken on any subject with passion, conviction, and pride. After that, I associated passion, conviction, and pride with Black people. I spent as much time as I was allowed down in the basement in Pat's tiny windowless room listening to the music of Sam Cooke and Billie Holiday among many other Black singers and musicians.

Upstairs my father and mother often were at loggerheads.

My father seemed to hate everything about my mother. Whenever she opened her mouth to speak, he looked miserable. Most of what she had to say was controlling and mean. Nothing was ever enough, the constant commands and her sour mood sucked up the air even in rooms with big picture windows. She could speak for hours on end without coming up for air or allowing the other person to say one word. Years later when I was an adult with a family of my own, I would time her diatribe/monologue. It was not uncommon for her to talk for 45 minutes without inserting a single comma. But, I could not put down the phone because every so often she would say in a loud rude tone, "Ya there? Ya there?" I would say, "uh-huh," and listen with no end in sight.

My father's complete emotional absence and my lonely longing for love all contributed to the predictable boy-craziness that set in around the age of ten. Lying around in my flared poodle skirt, cork-screw ponytail dangling, dreaming about boys and kisses was more compelling than any schoolwork.

The summer evening my father beat me with a leather belt began as a night of good fun. Bunny was thirteen and I was eleven. We were going to a movie at the exclusive beach club we'd recently joined. When the lights dimmed, I slipped away for a walk on the beach with a boy and did some "making out," a first in my life.

The film broke, and the movie night came to an abrupt early end. All the children were told to call their parents for rides. When Mother arrived, I was still missing. Presuming me drowned in the Long Island Sound, mother quickly organized a search party of children and parents.

When I was discovered lying on the beach kissing a boy, all juiced up on romance and adventure, my mother had already given the Coast Guard a description of my body so that they could identify my waterlogged corpse. All the way home she tore at her cheeks, screaming over and over, "This is your father's fault. He never does anything to control you!"

My father was home enjoying his solitude. Mother burst into the house locked and loaded, howling, "Do something about her! She's going to be a whore if you don't do something!"

"You want me to do something? I'll do something," he said as he took off his belt.

During the beating I felt very quiet and centered inside, thinking, "It's not my fault. I didn't do anything to deserve this. He's angry at her, not me. She's the one who caused this. Just put up with it. It will be over soon."

My mother got frightened and tried to stop it. "I didn't mean for you to hurt her," she said. She stood between us, trying to block the swinging belt before it hit and broke my flesh, a clumsy, slow-motion, violent game of monkey in the middle. I wondered why he didn't just go ahead and whip her. She was who he was really angry with, not me!

A neighbor heard the commotion and called the police. When they arrived, my father surprised me by dispensing with his usual proper manners. "This is not your business," he said. "It's a family matter." He slammed the door in their faces. They left. Those were different days.

I was failing every subject. I never did my homework. Whatever gives a person the ability to sit still and focus on work was completely missing in me. It might have seemed like willful rebellion, but it terrified me. I always knew the price, the disapproval and scorn I'd face the next day in school.

After a thirty-day stretch of undone math homework, the authorities finally called Mother in for a conference. Plunked in an uncomfortable chair, within earshot, I heard Mother weeping. Words like "incorrigible," "lazy," "limited," and "recalcitrant" floated through the closed door of the tiny office. I dissolved in a puddle of shame. Mother was very angry about the extra work she'd have to do to see that I caught up. I was twelve years old.

In the late 1950s, junior high school students were socially segregated. The upper-class White Jewish students, most of whom excelled in school, completely ostracized the Black kids from the projects. I cast my lot with them, they were outsiders too. The only thing about school I really liked was cutting classes to smoke, fool around, and listen to fantastic music in the bathroom with the "colored girls," a feisty and spontaneous bunch.

My seventh-grade language arts teacher was Black. His full name was Alfred E. Hampton, and he commanded such awe that students referred to him as Mr. Alfred E. Hampton, in the same manner as one might refer to F. Scott Fitzgerald or Franklin Delano Roosevelt. He was five feet tall, fat, with a thin moustache and dark skin. Mr. Alfred E. Hampton was so popular with all the students, White and Black, that it was a status symbol among the seventh graders if he ate dinner in your home. One day after a swim at the YMCA, I was surprised to see

Mr. Alfred E. Hampton watching television in the lobby with the other disenfranchised, disheveled residents. Mr. Alfred E. Hampton, a giant of a man, lived in the YMCA? This was where he went after school? Realizing that even the esteemed Black people lived in the projects, the tenements near the train station, or the YMCA was the beginning of my first inkling that Blacks and Whites were not treated the same.

When I was 14, living in White Plains, my first attempt at using oil paints failed. When I tried to mix the colors every color resulted in a different shade of poop. To solve the problem I loaded the colors directly from the tube on to a penknife and carefully smeared each separate hue onto the canvas.

The painting of 23 figures all with numbers for faces as well as numbers on their forearms were of old people, children, parents with their arms around each other, and a strange figure in the foreground, a flirtatious posed figure wearing a bathing suit resembling Marylyn Monroe. The point was to show no one was spared the fate of the European Jews, not even my film star idol. I put the painting in a closet and did not look at it for 60 years. A gallery in White Plains solicited works of art for a show about the Holocaust. My painting was accepted and hangs at this moment in a beautiful gallery in the town where it was created.

Over the years I looked without seeing. I perceived its meaning, for the first time, when it was hung on the wall of a prestigious well lit Gallery. 14 year old Susan Meltzer was trying to message me though time. One of the figures, an old gentleman, was a Black man. I never noticed before. The plight of the Jews and the Blacks were intertwined in my mind when I was only 14, by Pat, the "colored" girls, Mr. Alfred E Hampton and the Holocaust books.

I never read a word that was assigned in school, but I read piles of books on my own, devouring everything by authors I liked. I secretly imitated the reading habits of the well-behaved, studious girls who hung out at the synagogue youth center. In seventh grade, the smartest girl in our congregation was an avid reader. I yearned to be like her in so many ways; she seemed perfect, pretty and petite, and at the end of the school day she still looked as put-together as she had in the morning. I wanted to ask her how she stayed so tidy, but I never got the nerve. I could not publicly admit to caring.

Twenty-five years later, I looked her up. She had become a brain surgeon. I told her what she represented to me. "But, Susan, you didn't know me at all," she said. "Inside I was struggling too! Maybe I wanted to be more like you!"

I spent the majority of my time (when I wasn't in the bathroom) in the art room with Mr. H. He took an interest in me and encouraged me to draw and paint. On the last day of ninth grade I went to the art room to say goodbye to Mr. H. He grabbed me and delivered a big wet kiss, plunging his tongue into my mouth. My best friend came into the art room just at that moment. She declared loudly in Pig Latin, See-a–su-zzie ki-a-ssing, Misister Basares...roaring his name, which made him jump a few feet away. This incident ended my junior high school career.

Maybe it was enviable to be a disaffected, secretive intellectual. I didn't see it that way, it just kept me sane. I was a secret Shakespeare and Charles Dickens fan the way some girls worshipped boy pop singers. I cut school to spend days waiting in line to get a ticket to *Shakespeare in the Park*. I devoured biographies of jazz icons and everything Pearl Buck had written about China.

Quincy Jones once, regarding his lonely childhood with a schizophrenic mother, said that music was his mother, "and she never let me down." The old black and white movie version of *A Christmas Carol* was my mother. That film never let me down.

Channel nine's *Million Dollar Movie* used to show the 1951 film adaptation of Charles Dickens' classic three times a day, at nine, four, and midnight, during Christmas week. From the age of 11 through high school, I watched all twenty-one showings every year. Mother would wake during the wee hours, hear the television on, and crash though my reverie. "You're watching that movie again! Go to bed, it's not normal watching that over and over."

To me, Dickens' story about the industrial revolution expressed what I already suspected: wealth and status qualified the few, the rich, to judge the poor rather than to care, much less share.

People worked like rats, running for hours in treadmills to produce cheap energy, and could be abused, displaced and driven even deeper into poverty. Child labor laws were non-existent. Human beings were used. It wasn't the Westchester I lived in, but the connections were there, materialism and misery.

I was spellbound by the scene in which Scrooge awakens on Christmas morning a new man, a lover of life and everyone in it, humble, charitable, generous, compassionate, and deliriously happy. "That's what I want to be like when I grow up," I thought. The message that happiness is achieved by caring about the world wormed its way into my young psyche, deep and indelible. Ebeneezer and the three spirits influenced me to search for a way to change the world. My connection to Pat, and all Black American people and culture, was a foreshadowing but as a young girl I never imagined I would spend eighteen years inside of prisons.

My final grades at the end of my sophomore year in high school were five matching Fs. I even failed art class. I saved the report card, a cherished memento. It was the first year they were computer-generated—1963.

In my senior year I wrote a research paper on the tortured life of A.E. Housman, and received my first and only A+. But I had never made up those five failing grades so I didn't have enough credits to graduate. At the end of my senior year, I quietly stopped going. My high school career ended with a whimper instead of a diploma, parties, and proud parents.

Mother was very upset that I did not graduate from high school. She enlisted the help of one Sam Slotnick, "the only decent boy who has ever shown an interest in you," as she put it, to "try to talk some sense into your head."

Sam and I first met the summer I turned eleven, at the Beach and Tennis Club. It is entirely possible that he was part of the posse Mother recruited to search for me on that ill-fated movie night. I have no recollection of him from the summer of 1957, but he told me he remembered me; my lime green bathing suit, the boys following me around, my frequent excursions on eighteen-year-old Gary Lane's speedboat.

According to Sam Slotnick, I was the sexiest looking eleven-year-old he had ever encountered.

A few years later, my best friend Laurie Cimarosa and I ditched school whenever either set of parents was foolish enough to give us the family car. We'd go to New Rochelle and hang out in a pizzeria near the all-male Iona College. On one of these occasions, a fat, nerdy boy with a unibrow looming over horn-rimmed glasses approached our table.

"Do you remember me from the beach and tennis club?"

"No, I don't."

"I remember you; would you like to go on a date with me this weekend?"

In 1962, a girl went out with everyone who asked, just to be able to brag about to her friends about it. A boy you really liked got Saturday night, second best was Friday night, and anyone you didn't really like got Sunday afternoon. My first date with Sam was on a Sunday afternoon.

Sam and I went on a few more dates, but he wasn't "my type." He was far too sober and well-behaved. He took me to see Elia Kazan's *America, America* at the Pix Theater in White Plains in the middle of a snow storm. At every intersection, he slowed down and honked his horn, whether or not he saw a car approaching. The boys I considered "my type" would have sped up to try to get good skids going.

Now, home from Penn State University where he was majoring in bookkeeping, Sam took me out to Pat Foley's bar in downtown White Plains and made a valiant effort to deliver Mother's message: No man will ever marry you if you don't have a high school diploma. I couldn't believe I knew someone who would say something so un-cool. Marrying was not part of my plan.

With no job and nothing to do, I enrolled in night school in Manhattan, the goal being to get a high school equivalency diploma. I stayed up most nights watching television and chain smoking. At noon I left the house for the White Plains train station where I waited in the Kinney Rent-a-Car office for three hours until my train arrived at 5:05. The main attraction in the rent-a-car office was a handsome Black man in his thirties with brown skin and blue eyes. He introduced me to the music of Nina Simone and Nancy Wilson. One weekend I met him in Harlem. He showed me around, then took me to his apartment and seduced me. I was 17, old enough to consent. Even after the kiss from my art teacher, the Kinney Rent-a-Car salesman, and Mr. Leavit from camp Highmount, and the boy on the beach in Israel, I still did not know that attention from older men did not give me power. I was flattered, vulnerable, needy and an easy mark. Now I know I was a victim of a crime. The worse sexual abuse was yet to come. It would teach me an important lesson. People in pain cause pain. Many of the prisoners I later encountered were also victims of sexual abuse.

That year on my eighteenth birthday, I gathered up all my possessions and moved into the YWCA on West 45th Street in New York City. If it was good enough for Mr. Alfred E. Hampton, it was good enough for me.

The first night in New York, I stubbed my toe on the heavy door leading from Rhodes Preparatory Night High School into the street, ripping off a toenail. Then, stepping out of the bathtub, I gashed the bottom of my other foot on a razor I left on the floor.

The next day I set off to conquer Manhattan, wearing a white sneaker with the toe cut out on the right foot and a black high heeled shoe on the left. An employment agency sent me to a large engineering company in a high-rise office building. For eight hours, I filed cards by 10-digit numbers in an enormous room that held 175 desks, each inhabited by a female file clerk.

At 10:30, the coffee carts were wheeled in, and the women celebrated their fifteen minutes of freedom. I quit at the end of the first day. By law they had to issue me a check for the eight hours: $14. With no steady paycheck, even the YWCA would soon be beyond my means. But what time I did have to spend in New York, I spent feeling free and exploring the city. Freedom is precious and the men in my care longed to walk down a New York City street or ride a bus, with no one knowing who they were and where they had spent, for most, more than half their lives.

In night school, I met and fell in love with a boy from Mexico with the melodious name of Gonzalo Angel Ruiz Nava. His older brother was studying to be a minister at Union Theological Seminary located at 3041 Broadway. Gonzalo and I visited his brother there often. I met many serious Christians; I felt especially out of place since the Jewish Theological Seminary was directly across the street at 3080 Broadway. Gonzolo and I explored New York together until immigration authorities found him and sent him back to Acapulco on a Greyhound bus. His brother and I saw him off. I handed him my high school ring through the window of the bus, chased it a few hopeless steps with tears streaming down my cheeks. I was imitating a scene from an imagined Hollywood movie, very dramatic.

At age eleven, I'd studied at the Ballet Russe de Monte Carlo studio which was located on 53 Street between Fifth and Sixth Ave. I walked the same exact route at eighteen to get to night school. Saks Fifth Avenue, St. Patrick's Cathedral, Rockefeller Center, the sculpture of Atlas holding up the world; the sights between school and Grand Central were as familiar as the furnishings in my childhood home.

After a few months I ran out of money and had to move home and commute to school. I had an hour to kill before the train back to White Plains. I stopped to stand by the railing of the Rockefeller Plaza, looking down at the ice skaters and Christmas tree in winter, the fountain in spring and summer; as the sounds of Rachmaninoff's Second Piano Concerto played each evening at exactly 9:25. The lights and the movement of the skaters filled a crater that my spiritually bankrupt childhood had left.

Listening to Rachmaninoff's sacred music, I made promises to myself, a kind of secret ritual prayer:

* I'd never hit my children.
* I'd remember my thoughts and feelings, not go dead inside like adults.
* I would not forget my friends from the projects, or Mr. Alfred E. Hampton, or the Holocaust.
* I'd live inside my secret self, and never let the world destroy that unseen core.
* No spirits would have to take me on midnight voyages to set my priorities straight. I wanted to help people and care about the world like Mr. Scrooge when he woke from his sleep of unconsciousness.

Like millions of other young people in the sixties, I soon swapped my hoodlum costume for the latest style: day glow colors, tie dye, and high boots which I wore with confident swagger. I was living at home but escaped to New York on weekends.

I'd fallen in everlasting love with Black music back in Westchester, in Pat's room. Now I could spend Saturday afternoons at the Apollo Theater. I told Mother I was going to the Museum of Natural History.

For two dollars, I'd see the Saturday matinee film, plus the stage show featuring the best artists Motown had to offer. I saw *Lilies of the Field*, the movie that won Poitier an Oscar, and heard Joe Tex the same afternoon. Joe Tex stopped the show and thanked God that he, a Texas sharecropper, had made the journey from poverty to fame. He got a ten-minute standing ovation.

Mother found a ticket stub in my coat pocket punched at 125th Street. "What are you doing in Harlem?" she screamed. "Are you having sex with a Black person?"

To my amazement and delight, Mother listened when I told her how fantastic the shows were at the Apollo so she agreed to come along. The very next Saturday, we went: her in her current mink coat, white sneakers, and a turban, and me in a madras shirt, beads, and jeans. We actually had fun for a change. She loved it, even though she embarrassed me by spending the intermission walking up and down the aisles looking for Pat.

"Every Black person in the world isn't necessarily here," I told her.

"Well, you never know," she replied.

Harlem street fashion had a new look too. No more hair slicked flat with Vaseline and purple lipstick. The young people wore huge afros and bold African prints. There was so much hope among young people, Black and White in the 1960s. We believed it was the dawning of the Age of Aquarius which would bring lasting love and peace to the planet. It was our belief that we had the power to make a perfect world full of new possibilities.

My life felt full of possibility too. I got my night school diploma and considered what to do next. My plan, which seemed to me to be reasonable, was to become an expatriate painter in the south of France, have lots of affairs with fascinating men and paint pictures.

Mother took a dim view of this, and contacted an agency that recruited students for colleges that took anyone with blood flow and some semblance of high school.

I wound up in Charleston, West Virginia at Morris Harvey College, studying liberal arts.

Carolyn Allston, the only Black student at the school, invited me to spend Thanksgiving break at her home. The entire town consisted of a hollow between two defunct coal mines containing a row of shanties, a shabby general store, and a church, which we attended Sunday morning.

"Today is a special day, brothers and sisters. Today we are blessed with the presence of a little White girl, who is going to say a few words," said the pastor. "Thanks for inviting me. I bet I am the only White person ever to come here," I said. They laughed because it was true. I felt blessed to be welcomed so far from Scarsdale.

Morris Harvey had no campus infirmary; it was left to each student to find their own doctor. At a party, I met a "nice" Jewish doctor named Philip Ruben, the kind of man my mother would have hoped for as potential marriage material.

Summoned because I'd wound up hospitalized with a fever of 104, Dr. Ruben gave me a lengthy vaginal exam in full view of the hospital attendants. I had no symptoms to warrant a vaginal exam, as my diagnosis was mononucleosis. Mother came to bring me home. I told her about the public rape. She was devastated, but there was nothing either of us could do. Sexual assault awareness was nonexistent in that place and time. Doctors were gods. Now I had another older man who exploited me to add to the list.

That was the end of my Morris Harvey career. I've never been back to West Virginia.

Convalescing from mononucleosis back in Mother's micromanaged domain, I was all the more determined to escape.

I was full of enthusiasm for my future plans to make money and move to France. I registered my name with a ritzy babysitting agency in my old hometown of Scarsdale. I was sent to the home of a wealthy, beautiful 29 year old former fashion model. The agency described her as a housewife with two young boys. "Housewife" was hardly an apt term. She hired me full-time to replace her in the house. Several people were hired, each to relieve her of housewifely roles. In addition to a cook, a laundress, and a cleaning lady, she needed me to be the mother of her youngest son, who was mentality disabled.

The first time I saw her, she was pacing up and down a long indoor balcony, wearing a floor-length, brocade robe and a doctor's mask. "Germs!" she screamed , "the children have colds! Stay downstairs."

Everything downstairs was pristine and expensive. On the walls were paintings by a famous hard-edge painter who were in vogue at the time.

The first day I babysat, she left me with Steven, her disabled child. Along with the injunction not to get sick and to wear my own doctor's mask, she left me a long list of instructions. For dinner, I was told to cook beef stew with wine and minced olives. "No shortcuts," she said. "If you leave anything out, the children won't eat it."

"Where will you be?" I asked.

First she was going to a doctor's appointment. Then to a fashion show. Next, she was meeting a friend at the Bird's Nest, a restaurant in Lord & Taylor's. After that, she had her therapy appointment. Then she would be home to change her clothes for a dinner party in the neighborhood. I came to know over time that this was her typical day.

At 9 am, I would arrive, dress, bathe, and feed Steven. At 10:30, I would put him on the potty, where he cried for an hour while I held his hand. After that, we went to the playground, then home for a gourmet lunch, cartoons, more toilet time, a nap, and dinner. Another babysitter arrived in the evening.

I loved Steven, right through my boredom. I felt protective of him when a mother in the playground asked me about his "mental age", since it was obvious he was not like the other children his size. Some of the time, I sat around smoking and watching cartoons, especially if I worked the night shift when the mistress entertained dinner guests in her Kenneth Nolan designer evening gowns. Before a formal dinner party one night, she appeared in the nursery, wearing a hard-edged, black-and-white gown with enormous, ridiculous-looking butterfly-wing sleeves.

"You have no taste," she said, after she read my shocked facial expression. Were it not for Steven, I might have never found out at such a young age that I loved children more than adults. Were it not for the Model, I might not have understood how small and meaningless life can be for the rich and privileged

So a year passed saving money and toilet-training Steven. I enjoyed gazing at the long list of deposits piling up in my bank book. Soon I would have enough money to book passage to Europe and begin my real life.

Again my mother changed my life as she would do throughout my life. "Promise me, you'll try just one more time and I'll never ask again.

"Just apply to one college," Mother coaxed. "If you don't get in, then go wherever you want." She thought the State University at New Paltz would be a nice, safe place.

My D average in high school, my Cs at Morris Harvey, my 850 on my combined SAT scores, and a complete lack of recommendations made me confident I'd be rejected. Nevertheless, I still received an appointment for an interview.

I dressed for failure in a tie-dyed low-cut blouse and propped my knee-high combat boots on the interviewer's desktop. He advised me to put my feet down and asked me why I wanted to attend New Paltz College.

I didn't, I told him. We stared at each for quite a while until we both started to laugh. "Okay," he responded at last. "There's not much point in proceeding, but we may as well talk."

We talked for two hours. He took a bottle of wine out of a drawer and we toasted each other.

"To you, Susan, to your future," he said. "Whatever you do, you'll bring life to it. You've got something special to give. I hope you do develop it sometime. Consider becoming educated in the future—don't waste your talents."

Six weeks later I received a letter from New Paltz College and tossed it in the trash unopened. An hour later I heard Mother scream. When I ran downstairs, she was leaning over the garbage pail, clutching a piece of paper. "It's a miracle!" she said. "You've been accepted. You're going to be a teacher."

When I got to campus that fall and went to the admissions office to thank the man who must have pulled strings to change the course of my life, they told me he'd taken another job and wouldn't give me his contact information. I still think about him and wonder where he is and what he saw in me at such a difficult time when the only person who believed in me was myself. I am grateful to him every day. He inspired me to want to believe in people others had given up on, like the prisoners I would teach later on in my life.

New Paltz, it turned out, was far from the safe haven Mother envisioned. Downtown was a constant carnival of lunacy. A hippie named Tommy walked up and down Main Street with a live snake draped around his neck, wearing only a silk robe. An excommunicated Trappist monk lounged about in a long brown tunic, a large wooden cross dangling around his neck, ranting to anyone who would listen. An African-American man from the nearby city of Poughkeepsie could often be seen roller-skating around in a gorilla costume.

A national magazine rated New Paltz second only to Berkeley in marijuana consumption. My professors were busy chasing female students, getting stoned, and being "artsy" pretentious. "Maybe you have some talent," said hard-edge painter Joop Sanders, as he stood behind me and watched me draw, "but you will never be an artist. Soon you will marry, pop out some little ones, move to the suburbs, and become a middle-class housewife who changes diapers and never picks up a paintbrush again." His comment as well as his class taught me nothing.

Making art seemed to be a small aspect of art school. I received a four-credit A from a married professor named Harry for an "independent study"—for which I never did any work whatsoever, outside of my bedroom. I was still a mediocre student; Harry's A lifted my GPA to a 2.65, where it stayed until graduation.

One night, kind Sam Slotnick called me, crying. He'd flunked out of law school and his wealthy "good catch" of a fiancée had broken their engagement, since he was no longer husband material.

He was a nice guy, but still too "straight-arrow" with his tidy clothes and conventional values. I decided to turn him into a hippie with my tutelage and convincing skills. I invited him to come spend weekends in New Paltz.

We smoked weed and I told him to stare into the fire until he could no longer tell which was closer, the fire or the grate in front of it. This was to allow him to hallucinate which I believed was a good entrance into alternate states of reality. I believed I was an expert although I only took LSD once, which was enough alternate reality for me; a frightening, out of control experience.

I explained my paintings, gave Sam books to read, introduced him to people I deemed "cool." After a year of platonic visits, Sam told me he had enough. "If you invite me here again, I will take it to mean that you want us to have sex." Not a very romantic approach, so I forgot about Sam Slotnick, until I didn't.

A year later, missing him and not remembering those parting words, I invited him to a party.

"Get a room," he said. "I'll be there in exactly ninety minutes."

It was spring weekend. Every motel and rooming house was filled so I had an excuse not to have a room rented. At the party, we got high and went upstairs, where my THC-soaked brain discovered something fascinating: Dressed, he might look like Clark Kent, but nice, straight-laced Sam Slotnick became Superman when he removed his clothes. Naked, Sam shed his identity as Mother's good Jewish boy forever. After that, he began spending the weekends in New Paltz.

Driving down the Hutchinson River Parkway on our way to the Museum of Modern Art, Sam told me he was tired of conventional women who wanted nothing more than a wedding ring and a castle in suburbia. The perfect girl for him, he said, would support him in his dream of taking a trip around the world.

I have nothing in common with this boy, I thought, but in that very moment I had the strange conviction that I should marry him.

"It's your choice," Mother said. "You can have a magnificent white wedding at Temple Israel, with a world-famous caterer, Rabbi Gelb officiating, flowers from the Plaza Hotel, an expensive hand-embroidered dress, a makeup artist and hair stylist, and all your friends invited, or you can have five thousand dollars."

"I'll take the five thousand," I said

"No! You're having the wedding! It's my last chance to throw a big party."

I hated the wedding. Just for spite, I picked a bridesmaid who was 6 foot 7 to distract everyone during the peak moment when I walked down the aisle in the "the dress."

It was humiliating to wear a white dress, not because I wasn't a virgin, but because flower child me was so proud not to be one.

My mother and I came to fisticuffs screaming at each other on a Manhattan street over my disinterest in "saying yes to the dress." I said, "Yes" to every dress, which angered her. "Don't you care which one is right?" she asked.

"Not a whit," I said.

She cared. She told me she had a dream that it was her wedding and she was marrying Sam. For some inexplicable reason her dream opened my heart. Maybe it was because she never had a wedding party. As a girl during the depression she had so few material privileges, not to mention a dearth of attention and love.

Without my input, she hired a dressmaker in Hong Kong to make a re-embroidered Belgium lace wedding dress with dozens of little pearl buttons in the back. I would come to discover minutes before the wedding that the Hong Kong dressmaker made a devastating mistake. I had to urinate just before the ceremony. Mother and I were at hysterical loggerheads again in the bathroom when we discovered the inner slip under the dress was too tight to pull up over my hips. It took a long time to undo the dozens of little pearl buttons, pee, and refasten. The dress turned out to be more like a cage than a garment.

The wedding day began with the hair stylist and make-up artist futzing over me for hours until I wanted to bash both their heads into the floral arrangements ordered from the Plaza Hotel in New York.

In Jewish weddings, the bride does not attend the ceremonial rehearsal the night before the big day. I was instructed to stand behind a door. When it opened, my father would be there to guide me down the aisle. My husband would walk down a few steps, meet us halfway, shake my father's hand, kiss me on the cheek, and then Sam would escort me the remainder of the way to the altar.

Sam was stoned, so he fell down the few steps. My autistic father, in his confusion, shook my hand and kissed Sam on the cheek. The rabbi talked about the moon landing during the service. I did not know most of the guests, most likely people my mother wanted to impress. I married the nice Jewish boy mother wanted. Turns out it was the best thing she ever did for me.

We got married on December 22, 1968, the same day as Julie Nixon and David Eisenhower. I carried an Old Testament and a white rose, which was as inauthentic as I could be.

But the marriage has been every bit as authentic as the wedding was not. If I had married anyone else, I would not have become a dancer, artist, writer, and a volunteer inside prison walls. The men inside asked if my husband supported my spending so much time with grown men, in the intimacy created between dancer and choreographer. His trust meant the world to them. When they were released, many called Sam, thanking him.

Chapter 4

The World

Mark Twain said, "Travel is fatal to prejudice, bigotry and narrow-mindedness. The trip begins once you get out of your comfort zone. No one knows this until the adventure is underway. No matter how the trail is imagined it will wind up totally different. Lessons will be learned, some edifying, others exhilarating, many frightening." We'd survived Mother's dream, the Big Jewish Wedding. Now it was time for Sam's dream to come true. On August 14, 1969, the day before the Woodstock festival began, we boarded the Kranjebic, a Yugoslavian freighter bound for Morocco.

Waiting for us on the pier was a child who looked about twelve years old. In broken English he offered to find us a room, show us where to buy hashish, and, for a fee, to provide local street urchins for a sexual opportunity. He led us to a room for 50 cents American. It was dark with an earthen floor, a mattress with no box spring, and a hole in the corner for a toilet.

I was 23 and Sam was 25, two Westchester Jewish middle class kids in unfamiliar surroundings. In spite of our fears we put our overstuffed backpacks on the dirt floor and went with the child to buy hashish.

I have since learned that the brain's frontal cortex, the part responsible for making rational decisions and predicting consequences, doesn't fully develop until the mid-20s. Before that, making bad decisions can be really easy.

Most people, at that age, make their share of risky choices of varying degrees of severity and consequences. Almost all of the hundreds of prisoners I have known were between the ages of 18 and 25 when they were charged.

The boy led us through the narrow streets to a small dwelling. As we climbed a precarious winding staircase we met and locked eyes with an American soldier on his way down.

In a room at the top of the stairs, three older men sat on the floor next to an oversized ornate brass scale. The walls were lined to eye level with sheets of hashish. When asked how much we wanted, Sam indicated about a half inch wide and an inch high. The three men laughed together, pointing at us, seeming highly entertained by our naivete. "Give them the money!" I screamed at Sam. I wanted us to run as fast as we could down the stairs and into the street.

We gave them $10 and they gave us a small piece of dark brown pasty stuff the color and consistency of damp mud.

Once in the street, running, we realized that we had no idea which way to run to find the room with all our belongings. Soon we saw the street boy walking toward us.

"The man who sold you the hashish is in jail now!" he yelled.

We didn't know what that meant or what to do. We threw away our cubic inch of hash, which he promptly grabbed, and begged him to show us back to our room, which he did. We spent that night huddled together in a corner of the earthen floor waiting for the police to come and take us to a Moroccan jail.

By mid-morning the next day, we felt safe enough to venture out. We discovered another Tangiers, a recognizable metropolis with a nice, clean American Express office and a Holiday Inn. The street boy had led us to the old section, where all the filth and fear we had experienced the night before was replayed for incoming tourists each day.

We bought more hash, from a fellow American tourist this time. I dissolved it into a glass of tea. Within minutes I began a bad trip, way worse then the one time I tried acid. (That one had scared me out of ever trying acid again.)

As men in long draped robes passed the outdoor café where we sat, I was convinced I saw daggers and guns strapped to their naked bodies under their robes. It was terrifying.

As I was coming down, I was sure I saw Timothy Leary pass by our table and nod. "Oh my G-d," I said to Sam, "I think I just hallucinated seeing Timothy Leary." Sam, completely sober and lucid, said, "Yeah, he just walked by."

We headed across the Strait of Gibraltar to Spain on a ferry boat filled with gypsies and their sheep, lambs and goats. Our first night in Spain we camped out along with hundreds of big biting black flies. Sam wandered the grounds adorned in nothing but an Arab caftan with a hood. His resemblance to a biblical holy man was exacerbated by his typical state of mad-chill, a combination which imbued him with a faux Spiritual Look. (He was 25.) I, on the other hand, was scratching and complaining. We were quite the pair.

We hitchhiked through France eating bread and cheese, visited Monaco, then took a boat to the Balearic island Formentera, where we got hair cuts from a renowned London hairstylist and ate tapas. In Italy we saw Michelangelo's Pieta and prayed at The Great Synagogue of Rome on Yom Kippur.

From there we flew to Israel. I'd been there in 1967, only a few days after the war ended.

By 1970 the Wailing Wall had taken on aspects of a theme park, with flood lights and souvenirs. The houses that once blocked the approach to the wall were gone. I asked a young Israeli soldier, machine gun resting on his lap, "Where did all the houses go? Were the people relocated somewhere?"

"Who cares where they went? They were Arabs," he replied.

Steeped in the literature of the Holocaust, I'd believed it would be impossible for Jews to be indifferent to the human rights of another ethnic or racial group. Between a rich spiritual teaching and bitter experience, you'd think the Jewish people would know better. I had expected to find Israel a haven of compassion and justice. But along with the indifference to the fate of Arabs, I found that many Israelis discriminated against darker-skinned Mizrahi and Sephardi Jews from Arab countries. If the Israelis with only a blip in history separating them from the Holocaust could marginalize an entire population of people based on color, this could happen anywhere. Here in America we marginalize 3.2 million imprisoned souls, taking away all their rights of citizenship even after they've paid their debt to society.

From Israel, we took a ferry to Istanbul. We rode through the Near and Middle East in a rickety old bus stuffed with travel-worn international hippies, which made for long, draining days of unrelenting drudgery. From Turkey through Iran, across arid mountain range after arid mountain range, that creaky bus might have been driving circles around the changeless landscape of the moon.

We had crossed the Atlantic Ocean on a Yugoslavian freighter, shopped at the Kasbah in Morocco, partied on the beaches of the Costa del Sol, eaten in the cafés of Monaco, and hitchhiked to Rome. I had languished on Israeli beaches and snorkeled off the coral reefs in the Gulf of Aqaba. At every destination we searched for and found Chinese restaurants, then Jewish communities; world-wide, the Jews in the Chinese restaurants can let you know where the Jewish community is. We'd grown into fairly savvy travelers since being laughed at by the hashish barons.

In a cafe in southern France, Sam spread out the world map he carried in his back pocket and asked me to pick another destination.

I picked land-locked, lonely Afghanistan, since it seemed so remote, unfamiliar and exotic.

In 1970, Kabul looked as though everyone had just arrived the day before yesterday. People were in constant motion, toting things from place to place on unpaved streets. Nothing looked settled or rooted; all seemed continually in flux. The only building that stood out was a big warehouse labeled UNICEF, which reminded me of trick-or-treating in Scarsdale, then bringing pennies to school for starving children in places I'd never expected to go.

We found a decent hotel. On the wall of our room was a poster, a picture of a dead Israeli soldier being stepped on by a man in combat boots wearing a swastika armband. The peculiar, small, delicately lettered caption read, "The Jews are a strange people."

From Kabul we flew to Tehran, then on to the apex of the world tour, beautiful, mysterious, and seductive India. There I became aware of the censorship inherent in sanitized American culture. Deformity, hunger, sickness, death, even everyday human smells are kept behind curtains and closed doors, obliterated with chemicals. In India, there was no entrance or exit separating the truth of human spectacle from observation. There were humans so severely maimed that they looked like broken spiders crawling around the ground begging.

In America, real life blood and misery and grime are kept as much as possible behind closed doors, with only momentary glimpses revealed. This makes suffering scarier. The instant image, hidden, veiled, or framed by a sterile environment is like a short edit in a horror movie. Catch a glimpse, hide your eyes, open them to peer through your fingers and the image is gone, replaced by green lawns, shiny cars, and presentable people.

Not in India. I looked so long at suffering in India that it became known to me. Past the fear, I saw beautiful aspects. On the streets hundreds of people dwelled upon small patches of turf. But their meager belongings were neatly kept; accoutrements like flowers and pictures of religious deities were propped up in their tiny spaces.

The colors in India were like none I had ever seen anywhere. I remembered having wished for a larger palette when I was studying painting. The oil colors, rich as they were, were not enough. This took that feeling to a whole new level. Cerulean blue, thalo green, ultramarine violet all paled next to the colors that hit me in the gut the first time I entered a sari shop in New Delhi.

It took hours of tracing my fingers along silk fabrics, drinking in colors with a child's wide eyes, to finally make my choice. With my combat boots, jeans, and Afghani coat lying in a heap next to me, I stepped ceremoniously into my sari.

It was cream-colored with a wide strip of pink and a gold thread intertwined, running the entire distance of the border along six yards of cloth. To put the sari on was an art as intricate as origami. The fabric was folded and draped, folded and draped again around my breasts and my hips, until it hung as beautifully and looked as rich and majestic as a curtain in an opera house.

Sam bought himself a white Khadi suit, a comfortable pajama-like garment that kept the indigenous men looking both regal and cool in the hot Indian climate. In these disguises, we discovered the Great Mother, as India was often called by her patriots.

From New Delhi we took a train to Goa, a former Portuguese province nestled in a rain forest on the Arabian Sea. Renowned for its beaches, holy places, rich flora and fauna, and potent marijuana, Goa was a hot spot for hippies from all over the world.

The men of Goa sailed out to sea on old fishing boats at daybreak and returned at sunset. The women spent their days on the beach cleaning and salting huge piles of fish to be sold in the village's open market. It was an ancient lifestyle, a stark contrast to the dozens of naked, stoned denizens of the counterculture who now invaded their public space.

"Excuse me," a Goan woman asked, "could you please go over to that man and tell him that this is our home? We live on this beach. We are Christians, our children can see him, Please, ask him to cover himself!"

A tall, thin, pasty-white man with a fat spliff hanging from his lip stood about ten feet from the women and her children. "Damn uptight straight people!" he said when I conveyed her request. "No matter how far away ya go, can't get away from 'em!"

This woman was being classed with the teeming school of stockbrokers Jerry Rubin had dropped dollar bills on in 1967? Was this all that "Peace!" and "Make Love Not War" had come to, making people uncomfortable in their own homes? Neither psychedelics nor suffering conveyed the most basic recognition of other people's humanity and rights. "Who cares where they went? They're Palestinians!" "Who cares how they feel? They're straight people!"

The man on the beach and the Israeli soldier taught me that people with whom I share ideologies can be just as prejudiced as anyone else. From my community of progressives who champion social causes, I have heard, "Hahaha, you have a captive audience!" more than once. The prison dancers volunteer for the program. They are often ridiculed by officers and other inmates. It takes courage to dance in prison. By volunteering, they are executing one of the rights they still have, to avail themselves of opportunities to "become better men."

In some ways prisoners are our own occupied people. In jail, they become property of the state, with many rights curtailed. They no longer have a right to freedom, to bear arms, to free speech. They lose the right to assembly. They cannot vote while in prison and in many states they lose the right to vote even after they are released.

We bought a ticket with stopovers in Vietnam and Nepal and Burma, but I was too tired of traveling to go to all these places, and we flew directly to Bangkok. Sam wasn't tired. He could have gone on and on.

But the last of my joy in travelling to exotic locations would vanish after close proximity to the Vietnam War.

Waiting for us in the airport in Bangkok was the universal street boy whom we had grown so accustomed to seeing that we often searched for him among the multitude of people waiting for disembarking travelers, holding up signs with names on them.

He took us to a hotel in downtown Bangkok. After receiving his cut from the concierge, he gave us a set of instructions. "There are five floors in this hotel. Your room is on the second floor. You are the only guests on that floor. You can't go to the third floor or the fifth floor. That is off-limits to you."

As soon as I put my bags down, I took the elevator to the third floor, of course. The door opened to reveal Asian girls and American boys who looked like they weren't old enough to venture beyond American high school dances. The girls were running around half-dressed, giggling. One girl, maybe 12 years old, was sitting against a wall, crying, while an older girl scolded her.

"Get up!" the older girl screamed in English, "Or I'm going to have to get someone else."

American boys, also in various stages of undress, stumbled around drunk. They were astonished to see me there. Most had not seen an American female civilian since their tours of duty had begun.

A boy named Spanky after the boy from the Our Gang comedy series gave me a tour of the third-floor whorehouse.

"We're all combat soldiers on R&R from Vietnam. We have five days until we go back and have our heads blown off. As soon as we get here, the Mama-San fixes us up with a girl for the whole time. That girl, the girl sitting over there crying, she won't cooperate. She's my friend's girl. She's the third one he's gotten, another dud. Boy is he bummed out. They'd better get him someone good or give him back his money, that's all I gotta say. None of us has had any sleep--not any at all, not here and not in Nam. Here we've got a lot of partying to do--you know, in case it's the last time. Over there, most of us are too afraid to sleep. You know what I mean," he said, holding his finger to his head and making the universal gesture of murder by a firearm.

I stayed up with them all night. I talked to the soldiers, the Mama-San, the Papa-San, even the commanding officer, and finally to as many of the Asian girls as I could. All night, I kept talking with the boys, one after the other, while the sounds of sex and laughter created hour after hour background noise.

Each boy was entirely different and entirely the same as every other. Some were real patriots, ready to kill--no, anxious to kill--for democracy, while others were already speaking like the anti-war activists I'd spent hours planning strategies with back in college

Searching each face and hearing each story confounded my simplistic view of right and wrong, war and peace, good and evil. Until that night, I had thought the enemy was these boys. I had assumed they had made a clear-cut choice to go to Vietnam and kill when they could just as easily, I'd thought, have fled to Canada.

Many came from the southwestern United States, little towns with tidy Main Streets and, I imagined, churches on every corner. Canada, anti-war philosophy, not fighting for your country--these were ideas that had never entered their minds.

"My father went. My grandfather went," they told me. Some had fallen in love with the girls they had bought, and were full of plans after the war to rescue the naked damsels from their fate worse than death if they lived.

After Thailand, I wanted to go home.

We booked passage on a Chinese freighter called The Oriental Musician that was in the transporting 70 well-off retirees, older White Americans, around the world. We came aboard near the end of their six month journey.

For 40 days we sailed with the blue-blooded gentiles, watching them at dinner sipping their highballs and politely flicking their cigarette ashes in imitation crystal trays. They smelled of cologne, liqueur and smoke. The women wore heels and thick belts, straight skirts and silk blouses; the men's collars were too tight.

There were only 3 Jews on the ship: Abe Green, a middle-aged, retired man, and us. Just like in my favorite book "Ship of Fools," the three of us were isolated together at the far end of the dining room.

The most prestigious person aboard, the grandson of a famous politician, and his invalid wife were invited to dine at the Captain's table. The hottest topic among the passengers concerned who would be invited to the grandson's stateroom for cocktails before dinner.

On the fifth day of the voyage, Sam and I received the coveted invitation. The elderly grandson answered our knock on his stateroom door wearing a Central Casting rich guy get up, an ascot and a captain's smoking jacket.

He was smoking a pipe. In his hand was a Time magazine article about the lifestyle of hippies that he wanted to discuss with us.

"Do hippies really practice free love?" he wanted to know. I tried to broaden the discussion to a larger picture of who hippies were, but he kept bringing the subject back around to hippie sex lives, all he really wanted to talk about.

The next night, we got invited again. Did Sam and I personally believe in free love? Did we understand that because his wife was in a wheelchair that he could not have sex? He informed us that because Jews did not believe in an afterlife, or punishment by hellfire, that we were naturally more promiscuous than Christians. I didn't know that, I told him. Is that so?

The next time we were with him, he asked Sam if he could have sex with me. He would be happy to pay. "No," said Sam, finally dashing Grandson's dream of a wild night of fornicating with a Jewish hippie girl.

We became friends despite that awkward beginning. We continued to go to his cabin for cocktails and enjoyed all the gossip. On the last day of the voyage, he loaned us $20, since we had not a penny left after our long trip, and we parted with plans to meet again at his estate in Bronxville. Thus ended our trip around the world.

I met so many individuals on the trip; I would never have been able to understand were it not for proximity, which leads to intimacy. Without knowing what they wore, how they smelled, who and what they loved or hated, and more, all my opinions would be based on imaginings. One can never know someone from reading about them or seeing a film. So many assumptions turned out to be false.

When I first entered prison, I had assumptions about who the men confined there were. Just like on my trip, contact changes everything. After seventeen years and thousands of hours of contact, I have come to know them as they really were: human, like everyone else.

The Work Begins

I'd married in the midst of student teaching, which my professors had cautioned me not to do. The most meaningful moment, really the only meaningful moment from my student teaching experience, happened when I entered an art class at Lakeland Middle School in Mahopac, NY. Sixth graders were creating professional looking woodcuts with sharp tools rarely used by younger children. When I asked the teacher why she was giving these implements to students and why their work was so advanced, the answer she gave me has carried me through every teachable moment of my life: "Students will rise to the level of your expectations and no higher!" That has proved to be an ultimate truth.

Right after our world tour, I was employed as a social worker for the New York State Social Service division which ministered to unwed mothers and provided babies for adoption. I had only one client. She lived in a small basement apartment in Yonkers. It was obvious she was destitute, maybe the reason she was surrendering her third child for adoption.

I was supposed to ask many personal questions about her medical history, both physical and mental, her habits, drug taking and especially what she could reveal about the baby's father. Her mother, who was present for the beginning of the session, rose from her chair with great dignity and said, "I have never asked my daughter anything about the father. I will leave to respect her privacy and come back when called." I didn't even know a mother could be so respectful of her daughter. This was so beyond my own experience.

The social worker who was supervising me was seven months pregnant. I said naively, "That must help you with the clients. You are also pregnant. That might make them comfortable with you, since you have pregnancy in common.

She replied, "I would not talk about my pregnancy with those scum." My social work tenure did not last long.

Soon I was fired for crying and weighing myself. I was tasked with going to hospitals to pick-up newborns relinquished by birth mothers, drive the babies to the county office building and leave them there. Everytime I entered the office I was inconsolable and sobbing. I wanted to keep every baby. I also was addicted to the doctor scale, an obsession that began when my mother gave me diet pills in high school. Before the infant was brought to me, I often took advantage of the opportunity to weigh myself, finding a scale somewhere in the hospital. What a distinction! How many people besides me have been fired for two such bizarre reasons? To my knowledge, none.

I graduated with a BS degree in Art Education (BS is an apt term in my case), so I was certified to teach kindergarten through 12th grade art. After the wedding and prior to our world trip, we lived briefly in White Plains. I was hired at the Battle Hill Middle School in White Plains to teach art. Only five years after I flunked out of

White Plains High School, I attended orientation day as a newly hired teacher. Most of my high school teachers also attended. I was introduced to the entire district-wide staff as Mrs. Slotnick. Inside I was still Susan Meltzer and my looks had not changed much. Although many of my former teachers said I looked familiar, none realized who I was until I told them. They were pleased and surprised that I "turned out so well."

Beginnings do not always determine outcomes. Recently I read an article in the news about a former prisoner who became a lawyer and is now a professor at Yale University.

Back in New Paltz, Sam and I tried to keep a global perspective. Our apartment was decorated with fabrics from India and Taiwan. I cooked all our meals in a wok, using Indian and Chinese spices, and we ate on the floor, scooping food in our hands Indian-style.

Within a few months I became pregnant, which amazed me and consumed my thoughts. Mother wasn't at all impressed. "Anyone can have a baby," she said. "Anybody can get pregnant. How long do we have to talk about it?" I should be "normal," she said, and take pregnancy more in stride.

On the way to the hospital it was snowing, soft tiny snow, glinting under the streetlights. I focused on breathing and rubbing my belly in wide, circular motions, feeling calm, not my usual self at all. Still, the pain was excruciating. With each contraction, my back felt as though it were being severed by an ax. Why hadn't anyone told me how horrible this would be?

Between pains, I thought of all those multitudes we'd seen, walking, eating, getting off trains, each single one of them a product of someone's suffering, a breathing result of some frightened, wide-eyed woman enduring this, rising to meet an occasion so challenging that she would never be the same. It made me love all women.

Soon they showed me a little pink, black-haired, red-flushed creature with a punched-in face, and then they whisked her away. It was unusual to feel so much sudden love, a mystery.

Mother came to visit, intent on getting me to appreciate her latest sacrifice; she had gone to our apartment and put the crib together. "I worked like a dog! My back is killing me," she told me. "I'm going to stay with you for the first few days, and if any of your hippie friends smoke around the baby, I'm kicking them out. I want to make this clear. Do you understand me? There isn't going to be any parade of visitors. If there is, if you don't do what's right, I'm leaving."

We fought. The young woman in the next bed began to cry. "My mother's dead," she said. "What's wrong with the two of you?"

Rebekah and I left the hospital wearing homemade matching kimonos, a black and red Indian print. "That hippie girl dressed her baby in black!" said the scandalized nurses.

Baby Rebekah and I went on long treks through the mountains. Sometimes I'd take her off my back when we were deep in the woods and make a bed of pine needles for her to nap on. Sam shared the child-care and housework without complaint, and supported whatever I needed to do, whether it was dance, paint, or visit my friends. Soon I was pregnant again.

My best friend Ruby was a charismatic, beautiful thirty-nine-year-old and a practicing lay therapist supervised by a local psychiatrist who was also her lover. A renowned womanizer, it was rumored he was having sex with his patients. Ruby and I would walk and talk, about my baby, new pregnancy, and her grand passion, the psychiatrist. "You shouldn't be having another baby unless you're madly in love with your husband," she said. "I'm risking it all—my family, my children, my reputation—to follow my heart. I'm going to give myself totally. Every shred of me is for him. I'm saving nothing."

"You'd better save something for yourself," I said. "You might need it."

At my eleven-week prenatal checkup, the doctor could not find the baby's heartbeat.

Patients who miscarried were put on the maternity ward; newborn babies were wheeled to and fro throughout the day. I marveled at how other women took their loss in stride. I was a hysterical wreck, a raw mass of emotion. When the nurse asked me to fill out the fetal death certificate I sobbed. Mother's voice rang in my ears. "Why must you always be so emotional?" I envied the others their numb calm.

Then I had an epiphany, a moment of self-love that would take me through many heartaches. What I need to take in stride, I realized, was that I would never be able to take anything in stride. Since then, I have not been able to take injustice—especially in the prison system—in stride, although I have learned through my own losses to manage my emotions while serving my students' needs.

I called Ruby to tell her that the baby died. The day after my miscarriage she shot herself though the chest and was discovered after school by her eleven-year-old son. The relationship with the doctor ended; the catalyst for the downward spiral leading to her death.

My miscarriage and her suicide began a saga of expensive obstetrical failures lasting for seven years. For whatever body-mind reasons, the shock of losing my baby and my friend's death shut down the woman part of my biology. I stopped menstruating for seven years.

My mother intervened with a suggestion that cured me.

A Catholic priest told me that God worked through my mother despite our horrible relationship. She pushed me to go to college, to marry Sam. She has at times been an agent for good in my life, but in the moments of contact often her good intentions disappeared in the face of her narcissistic needs.

After my father died, Mother lived in a condominium in Florida; brown and grey furnishings among white tiles, mirrors, and glass everywhere. To please her I also had white tiles installed on my kitchen floor. Daily, I got down on my hands and knees to wash and scrub the white floor.

Sometimes while washing the white tiles, memories came to mind of times she tried to be an agent for good in my life. In college I received a letter.

To my daughter Susan,

Although I have never told you, I love you very much. You are dear to me because you have long thick black hair just like my mother did. I loved her more than anyone in the world. That's why I love you daughter dear, because you remind me of my beloved mother.

From your father, Jack Meltzer

I carried this letter with me for years.

I was a sophomore in college when, during spring break, I came home to find that my father had moved to a hotel next to his record store. Mother was hell-bent to get me to take her side. Her filibuster lasted for hours late into the night, a diatribe of complaints about my father, some of it much too personal for a daughter to hear. In a desperate attempt to get me on her team she said, "And that letter you carry around with you from your father, he never wrote it—I did!"

A therapist told her my father's lack of love was the cause of my problems. The letter was her attempt to be parental but that impulse was weaker than her need for agreement. From my mother I have learned that even the best of intentions cannot trump our weaknesses.

She was deprived of love and abused as a child. She never recovered. It has taken six decades for me to have compassion for her. No one ever hurt me as much as she did. Feeling compassion for her was difficult. Once I could, compassion towards the men in the prison—even those who committed heinous crimes—became possible.

I no longer define my mother by a litany of painful incidents. The totality of a person should not depend on one or more bad choices, made from faulty thinking and weakness. No one is all one thing.

Although Mother did not understand why I wanted a second child, her suggestion of a cure gave me one. She told me to embark on a "complete cleansing fast," taking only water for at least 25 days.

I went to Pawling Health Manor, a vast Victorian-style mansion with dozens of bedrooms. In 1950 Dr. Gross opened a resort devoted to curing illness through fasting. By the time I arrived, the primary focus was weight loss, with only a few clients with serious health issues.

All but two of the other clients were there to lose weight. One woman stood out. She wasn't glamorous and chatty like the others. Every morning she practiced tai chi by the outdoor pool. I was struggling to read *In Search of the Miraculous*, by P.D. Ouspensky, the Russian mathematician and esotericist known for his exposition of the work of esoteric teacher George Gurdjieff, whom I myself discovered when I was about forty-five. When she got a glimpse of the title she told me she had been a student of Ouspensky.

Apparently the miraculous had come and found me, in the person of Joy Dillingham, the founder of the School for Practical Philosophy in Manhattan. She offered to help me comprehend the book, and with each daily lesson, she unpacked more of Ouspensky's ideas.

"You have to continue all your life, or you get stuck in a no-man's land between ignorance and a truly examined life. It's a purgatory to be between these two points," she said.

Miss Dillingham told me that a man named Frank was teaching "the work" near New Paltz. "I have many reservations about him; I don't know if I'm going to allow him to continue teaching through my school," she said. "He's no longer really serving the method. I believe he is serving himself. When I've solved the problem, I'll tell you how to connect to the group in your area. Until then, continue on your own. You're very talented."

Talented! To me, talent had always meant being able to sing, dance, or sketch. What talent did she see?

I lost seventeen pounds in seventeen days. When I went home, the whole house smelled like an opened spring flower. I had no idea where the smell was coming from until I found a blossom dripping with sap at the top of a tall plant we'd had for years that had never before bloomed. The flower grew and bloomed during my fast. That was thirty-three years ago and we still have the plant. It never bloomed again. Shortly after I came home from my fast, I became pregnant with my second daughter, Sarah Ariel, the miracle child.

Miss Dillingham called and told me that the recalcitrant Frank had been ousted. Although it was against policy, due to my "talent" I would be allowed to attend a "work" group that had been meeting for several years. The atmosphere was formal, the straight-backed chairs precisely arranged, flowers on the small table at the front of the room beside the teacher's elevated seat. The students moved and spoke slowly and deliberately, guided by some unspoken internal rule. Clothes were conservative. We sat upright, legs uncrossed, listening to the teacher who read verbatim from notes.

After a few classes, the droning two-hour recitations began to put me to sleep. The whole point was to wake up from the "sleep of unconsciousness," so I quit.

Months later, a promotional coupon offering a free massage came in the mail. The masseuse recognized me instantly. "I was in the Gurdjieff work group you came to a few times," she said. "We all believed that you were a spy, sent by Miss Dillingham to gather evidence against Frank. Frank is a better teacher. Miss Dillingham asked us to give the new teacher a chance, but he was so ineffective compared to Frank! We've all defected."

Not wanting to wind up in purgatory, halfway between ignorance and realization, I asked to meet with this Frank. I was told to come to the college science building the next Sunday night.

When I arrived, the building was dark, all the doors were locked.

"Are you Frank?" I asked the skinny man walking toward me.

"Yes," he said. "Has somebody unlocked the building for us?"

"No," I said, "but follow me, I'll try to find us a way in."

Frank was amused. "I'm a follower of Susan," he said to the student who showed up with the keys.

We sat across from each other in a small, windowless room, surrounded by displays of vegetation and animal life of the Paleozoic era. "You can ask me anything that you want," he said.

"Aren't you afraid to lead people down a path as dangerous as this one without a teacher of your own to guide you?"

For several minutes Frank leaned back in his chair, his closed eyelids fluttering. When he spoke, it was deliberate; he chose his words with care. "I live on a small inheritance from my family, so I am teaching people only as a service to them, without material gain."

Other students joined us. Frank taught without a script. He slipped off his shoe and then tried to ram his foot into it without untying the laces, demonstrating the unconscious way we treat our possessions, showing though this simple example how the ego tries to get away without honoring the laws governing the universe. From the smallest law to the largest, sleeping humanity is a danger and the "work" is to wake up. One time, a student asked a question about the Holocaust. "Never use the phrase 'man's inhumanity to man," Frank said. "Every action committed was human because a human being did it. When you encounter a holocaust, a murder, the abuse of a child, say to yourself 'and this too is human.' Thus, you will have compassion even for everyone." I would never forget those words especially when I was confronted with Rivera's crime. Because of what I learned from Frank I was able to simply say, 'Take off your shoes, it's time to dance.'"

The "work" was all-consuming. Frank was very demanding. He took a risk making life decisions for students who believed he was on a higher level of being then an ordinary person.

As soon as you reached a new level of devotion he upped the ante; expecting you to work harder, spend more time; then the demands increased again. I stayed up all night transcribing three hours of notes from memory. Although I could not do simple meditation exercises, he had me teaching classes. I brought in dozens of new students, increasing revenues.

When my third daughter, Elianah Kol, was born, the incessant demand to "put the work first" became too much. Frank visited me in the hospital two days after the birth, saying, "Okay, you've proved your point; it's time to get back to the work." I developed colitis. I went to the doctor and took the medicine without results. I read in some new-age health book that colitis occurred in people who were under tremendous stress and needed to make decisions between inner and outer conflicts. Normally I would say, "Phooey!" Not this time.

I quit. It was clear he was hurt and disappointed. That day, the colitis disappeared, and never returned.

In the prisons, and in dozens of other situations, I taught the concepts and truisms I learned from Frank, to extraordinary results. What

I did not do was allow any student to put me on a higher level. The people I taught, once they saw positive change, had a propensity to think of me as a "guru."

"Please don't put me on a pedestal—it's a very shaky place," I told them. We learn lessons, positive and negative, from our teachers—who to be, and who not to be.

Chapter 5

Little Girl Dancing

As a little girl, I wanted to dance ballet. At eight years old I read a book about famous ballerinas, and the story of Cuban ballerina Alicia Alonso captured my imagination. From an early age, Alicia was partially blind. Lights on different parts of the stage were used to guide her to her partners.

She fell in love and married at sixteen, and her vision worsened, requiring surgery. She was ordered to lay completely motionless in bed for an entire year without moving her head, chewing too hard, laughing or crying. If she didn't comply, she risked losing her vision forever. Her husband, also a dancer, sat with her for hours every day, using his fingers to tap out steps on her body, teaching her the great dancing roles of classical ballet.

"I danced in my mind," Alonso wrote. "Blinded, motionless, flat on my back, I taught myself to dance Giselle."

I aspired to her greatness, but my will was weak. I didn't have it in me then to work hard and comply. I wasted an exceptional opportunity. My teacher at the Ballet Russe de Monte Carlo school on West 45th Street was Madame Youskevitch, the wife of Russian ballet star Igor Youskevitch. Too young to appreciate her, I'd stop trying and lean against the barre the moment she looked away.

And after two years of ballet study, the boy-craziness kicked in with all its juicy promise. I fell in love with hip shaking and the heat of dancing with a boy. Ballet dreams were shrugged off. Failing in school, my relationship with Mother in constant turmoil, my father emotionally nonexistent, and my siblings facing one challenge after another, I felt suffocated in sadness as puberty turned to adolescence.

Dance was there for me, a constant lover as no boy could be.

I stayed home on days when Mother was leaving the house and danced for hours on end. I'd fake a fever, the old thermometer-on-the-light-bulb trick. Once I had the house to myself, I would go into the living room, pull down the shades, pick my favorite music from a pile of 45 RPM records and dance in my pajamas all day. By the time the others came home, dancing had worked its reliable magic on my mood. My circumstances were unchanged, but I was different. Free. I taught myself that dancing could make a person who was not free, either from a real or metaphorical prison, to feel free, even if only momentarily.

In college, I had a favorite partner. I first saw Tom in the college art building, both of us toting metal tackle boxes full of small tubes of paint. He was a fellow art education major, a self-taught pianist, a calligrapher, and he could dance. He'd grown up in a working class Italian family in Bensonhurst, Brooklyn. His father was scornful of his creative nature. We were well-matched in alienation from our families of origin.

On weekends we'd dance all night. He could lead, and I could follow. The dances were invented as we went along, so attuned were we that we never did the same dance twice. Other dancers would clear the floor and gather round to watch. The connection with Tom, which I mistook as romantic, came from the power inherent in moving with another in unison. Generals know that marching soldiers moving in unison to music feel indestructible. This is a historic and universal way to manipulate young men to go into harm's way.

In the prison dance program, the men often talked about how choreography done in unison gave them a special connection and feeling of power.

Tom and I spent afternoons in the music department piano cubicles, me sitting beside him, soaking my brain in his improvisations, his fresh, dissonant harmonies. He knew about my history with *Exodus* and often played the movie theme.

Thanks to long hours in the soundproof booths at my father's record store, lost in the magic of Etta James, Ella Fitzgerald, Nat King Cole, all the greats in the American songbook, I had a vast mental library of lyrics. My absolute favorite was "That's All," with its evocation of timeless, forever love.

Dreams of dancing my way through a musical marriage imploded when an anonymous letter revealed to me that Tom was gay. Years later, he confessed to me that he'd written it himself.

We danced together again, ten years later, meeting by chance at a bar. Then another decade passed before, jogging across an old railroad trestle on a wooded trail, I found Tom sitting on a bench with his head in his hands. He was dying of full-blown AIDS.

I asked him if there was anything I could do. "I always wanted to rent a concert hall with a baby grand and have a real piano recital- a hall full of people, me in a tuxedo…"

All it took for me was one phone call to head the music department who provided the hall, with the baby grand included. The dancers of my first youth company, dressed in their finest, stood at the door giving out programs. My dear old friend ended his performance with "That's All," the lyric promising love forever. There's more than one kind of love that can last forever, and more than one way to keep a promise.

I promised myself to keep dance in my life. At the time I had no plans or aspirations to become a dancer or make dance my avocation. I didn't need to plan. My life was going to lead me there and all I did was follow it.

When Sam and I settled back into New Paltz after our world tour, in my path appeared another great teacher, Brenda Bufalino. Brenda was a world-renowned teacher of tap, modern, and Afro-Caribbean dance. She founded a New Paltz studio she called the Dancing Theater. For the next several years I attended her classes several times a week. Brenda was demanding, sometimes caustic, always dedicated.

I had doubts at first. At age twenty-five, I was far too old to become a professional dancer with a competitive technique. "Do what you love," said Brenda, "and it will lead to something if you just pay attention and have some faith."

I started teaching exercise and stretching, charging three dollars a class. When Rebekah was nine, I began teaching a children's dance class for her and her friends. In retrospect, I was a half-baked teacher. Teaching adults, most of my attention was spent watching myself dance in the mirror while the other women imitated my movements. I knew very little about teaching dance. To my surprise, the class became popular.

I patterned my teaching on the methods of Jacques d'Amboise, one of the finest classical dancers of our time. He'd begun the National Dance Institute for public school children. Formal technique was not required. The students looked terrific, had a blast, and performed entertaining shows without even removing their shoes. In my class, word spread, and I was hired to teach dance at a local private school. I also founded my own dance school called FiguresInFlight. Each year I choreographed and directed an extravaganza I called "Dance-A-Matazz," with flashy costumes, hundreds of dancers, and overflowing joy. We packed the theater. Audience members danced down Main Street afterward.

It never crossed my mind to craft serious dances, or to prepare children for dance careers. After five years of producing Dance-a-Matazz, I told my most talented students that if they aspired to performing careers they needed to go somewhere else and find a "real" teacher.

"Why don't you go somewhere and become a real teacher?" asked one of the students, and so I did. For nine years, every Tuesday, I took the Trailways bus to the Clark Center for the Performing Arts in Manhattan. Established by Alvin Ailey in 1970, the school offered jazz, ballet, modern, and a variety of African and other ethnic traditions. World famous teachers like Alvin Ailey, Fred Benjamin, Pepsi Bethel, Thelma Hill, Mary Hinkson, Carmen de Lavallade, and Anna Sokolow all taught there at one time or another.

Thelma Hill was a brilliant teacher of the Lester Horton technique. Horton had developed his own approach that incorporated elements of Native American folk dance, Japanese arm gestures, Javanese and Balinese isolations for the upper body, and Afro-Caribbean polyrhythms. There's an emphasis on clean lines, unrestricted dramatic freedom of expression, and ballistic, powerful movements.

Forced off the stage by injury in the 1960s, Thelma's teaching career had flourished; her students referred to her as "Mother Hill" because of her compassion and generosity. By the time we met she was past middle age, and quite overweight. She wore stretchy polyester pants suits to every class. No matter what color her pants were on a given day, the right pants leg was shorter; her clothes were handmade from a lop-sided pattern. Her lack of self-consciousness and total focus on her students taught me that watching myself in the mirror was wrong and would have to stop.

I was too old, from out of town, part of a small White minority, and not able to keep up. Thelma would often come over to me in the middle of class, put her hand on my chest, and say, "Take it easy, you're working too hard."

Then, on what started as an ordinary Tuesday bus ride, I opened my *New York Times* and saw a surreal headline. "Renowned teacher, choreographer, and dancer Thelma Hill died last night of smoke inhalation caused by a fire in her New York apartment." My bus had just passed the Newburgh Thruway exit. Thelma's class would have begun at 10 AM, followed by Pepsi Bethel's jazz class at noon.

Stunned, I pushed the reality away. All I let myself think was finding a Lester Horton class to take from 3:00 to 5:30.

I found one, taught by famed choreographer Joyce Trisler. I knew the class was above my level, but it was the only one I could fit into my schedule and get home in time to see Rebekah before she went to bed. After fifteen minutes of struggling with the exercises, Trisler came up to me and said out loud, "Go home, you shouldn't be dancing."

To which I replied, "Go home, you shouldn't be teaching." That's when the heartbreak really hit. Mother Hill was gone, and irreplaceable. Now I would teach myself, with independent study, just like I had in high school. Just like the prisoners.

My brother Steven was working in a video store, and made a tape of every dance number from every film they had in stock. I watched it over and over, making lists of all the dance moves that appealed to me. When Channel 13 broadcast *Dance In America*, I recorded that too. For hours I would study the steps, repeating each sequence until the physiology and dynamics were drilled into mind and muscle memory.

Teaching myself the great modern dance pieces of Alvin Ailey, Martha Graham, and Paul Taylor took many months. I developed a method I used for years: after learning each piece, I videotaped myself, noted corrections, fixed the problems, videotaped myself again... repeated dozens of times. It reminded me of memorizing all of A.E. Housman's *A Shropshire Lad*, of reading all the Holocaust books. The nucleus was repetition, the impetus was passion. Studying alone seemed to drive the mastery deeper.

My students at FiguresInFlight, 150 of them at the peak, were becoming technicians. I was attempting to expand my choreographic horizons. My first "serious" pieces did not tell a story or even have a narrative line; choreography meant putting together aesthetically pleasing combinations, moving the bodies around on stage using the same criteria a painter would: harmony, variety, and texture, to be a moving collage.

My most successful piece was *Lands of Fire*. A musical departure, it was choreographed to a South American instrumental composition. A dancer with impressive credentials, knowing my background, remarked, "I was watching it and wondering where you learned (she named some choreographic tactic)?" She'd studied in composition class at NYU.

"I probably picked it up from watching an old MGM musical."

I kept heading down to the Alvin Ailey Dance Center when I could manage it. I still felt that my students deserved and needed to study with more accomplished teachers, so when a young African-American teacher named Earl Mosely told me, "I really enjoyed your presence in my class; you seem to know what you're doing," I followed him out of the studio and asked if he'd spend the month of July teaching my students. After class with the students, Earl taught me. Every session was videotaped, and I used those tapes for many years.

Great teachers became our summertime tradition, each one bringing me new skills. It was a great chance to talk shop with other teachers and choreographers, mull over the abilities, strengths, and weaknesses of each student, and devise a plan for helping them during the year ahead.

I'm still no academic in the world of music or dance. Some choreographers can just look at a musical score and understand the time signature. I count everything cock-eyed; I can't tell you how many beats are in a bar. Choreographers should be able to retain steps, and typically have a broad and deep knowledge of different dance techniques, including historical and contemporary styles. I knew one modern technique, some ballet, and a smattering of Jazz and African dance. I developed a skill set of my own: quick thinking, creative ideas, a painter's visual acuity, teaching skills, stamina, perseverance, passionate love for the dancers, and intense motivation.

My closest friend at the time was Livia Vanaver, a dancer/ choreographer with encyclopedic knowledge of music and dance forms from all over the world. Livia was everything I wasn't, technically proficient in many modern styles and ballet, and a beautiful dancer herself with an advanced degree in dance and dance education. She was often hired to conduct residencies in schools. Just the phrase "artist in residence" filled me with admiration. When a school principal who attended one of the Dance-A-Matazz shows asked me to come and conduct a dance residency, I was stunned.

"Me? I don't know dance from all over the world or how to teach creative movement! What would you want me to do?"

"Just do what you do with kids," she said. "I love your work with children."

Without much in the way of a plan, I found myself in a third-grade room in the diverse and downtrodden little village of Ellenville, across a mountain from New Paltz. I found the teacher attempting to teach while the students looked out the window, fidgeted, and fooled around. How could any learning take place if the students weren't holding up their half of the bargain, paying attention? On the spot, I began to translate Gurdjieff's concepts into third grade language.

"What did you ask your parent or whoever was taking care of you to do every time single time you jumped into a swimming pool?

"Look at me!" a chorus of third graders yelled.

"Why did you want to be looked at over and over again, even if the person who was caring for you had seen you jump twenty times already?"

"Cause when they watch I know they care. They love me."

"Attention equals love," I pointed out. "You can't love anything without first directing your attention towards it. Attention is the verb in loving, so simple yet we don't know that. Moving your body and directing your attention are your only powers. Don't let other kids steal your power by distracting you from your schoolwork.

"The harder you work at something, the less boring it becomes. When you're bored it's because you're boring, kids who are bored need to lengthen the list of what interests them." My assistant and I dramatized it in roleplays. How much fun is a playmate that answers every suggestion with, "I don't want to do that, it's boring!" That playmate is boring; if you're bored, then you're boring!"

"You can do two things at a time, but you can only pay attention to one. Raise your hand if you ever read a whole page in a book and actually read every word and didn't know if it was about grasshoppers or nebular fission?" All hands, including the teacher's, were raised.

"Success comes when you do what you don't feel like doing. You become what you practice. If all you do in school is fool around, by the end of the day, you're a bigger fool. If you pay attention to being kind, by the end of the day you're a nicer person and a better friend."

The impact of the material on the children took me by surprise.

From a parent:

> I just wanted to write to tell you that Nick is so impressed by the dance class that he is taking this week, and I am amazed at the lesson that this is teaching him. In my opinion, it is the BEST thing he has ever learned in school. He said to me that "attention, is love"—that you can't love anything without giving it attention. Or truly accomplish anything or be focused on anything without giving it full attention. I believe that this lesson will stay with him the rest of his life.
>
> If he learns nothing else in his entire grade school experience but this, he has come out a better person and someone who will accomplish great things. I don't know what this program is

truly about; I can only tell you that it has had a profound effect on my child. Thank you for changing Nick's life in such a wonderful way.

The powerful reaction to the "attention through dance" core that I had invented on the spur of the moment was overwhelming. A woman with an autistic daughter fell into my arms weeping; she said her daughter's autism was gone while she danced. The girl stood still, paid attention, for the first time in her life.

I found that within minutes I could pick out which child was emotionally challenged, had a physical limitation, was at the top or the bottom of the class, the school clown, or had been abused. The teachers told me I was a mind reader with uncanny powers to see immediately who each child was. All I did was pay attention, that's the key to insight.

A boy who the principal predicted "would probably wind up in prison" took to dancing, and wanted to continue after the residency ended. His cousin, a student at an alternative school for disruptive children, wanted to join him. Neither of them had money or transportation to come to New Paltz and continue dancing in my private classes. I believed that if they could keep dancing the outcome of their lives would change. I paid for a weekly taxicab for the sixty-mile round trip. Frank taught me to go to the nines in the service of the students, which I did.

The residency is the best thing that has ever happened to me in my life. It's so spiritual I can't explain. Susan has taught me to show my spirit, when I dance I get an incredible feeling. I feel like I am letting my true personality shine through, for everyone around me to see. I never met anyone in my life like Mrs. Slotnick, so much faith in me, I learned to control myself, not be afraid to shine.

Jennifer, grade five

FLIGHT

Dear Ms. Slotnick,

My son Corey who is in Mrs. Gantz's fourth grade class at Rosendale Elementary has done nothing but talk about you. I have never seen him so enthusiastic or serious about anything. Every night he shows me the steps over and over. The look on his face while he is dancing is priceless, he says you are so kind, so cool, and you must know what a compliment that is from a boy his age. Never in Corey's school experience have I ever seen him so excited about any one or any activity like he is about the residency.

Sincerely,
Mrs. Brainard

At the final residency performance, audiences were always impressed with how focused and in unison the children were after only five hours of instruction. Parents would tell me the dancers in the residency looked more trained than the dancers at the end-of-the-year recitals in local dance schools.

After a performance at the Lake Avenue School in Saratoga Springs, a woman asked me if I took "disciples." Another woman, a dancer, said she'd just returned from London where she saw all the latest shows, and the residency performance—after only five hours' practice for each class—she said was better.

With such over-the-top feedback, and my damaged academic history, I had to fight grandiosity. Grandiose delusions are charac-terized by fantastical beliefs that one has magic powers, and are often spiritual in nature. This can indicate psychosis, and for one awful, agitated day, the wounds on my ego got the better of me and I was sure that I was special, with special powers.

I knew that hallucinating about myself would have a corrosive effect on the residencies, as well as my psyche. When Livia told me that I was the most talented person she had ever met, I believed it. To bring myself down a few notches I reminded myself that talent is cheap; most people have several. Developing talent is rare. I was talented, and so what? It wasn't mine to claim; it was no more meaningful than having thick dark hair or blue eyes, a birth accident. What could be claimed was the work. What could be claimed was the application, the focus on making a better world though the application of my talents. To be a good Jew one has to accomplish *tikkum olam*, the Hebrew term for healing the world. My agenda: to do this one dancing child at a time.

School principals kept calling, inquiring about the "attention residency." To date, over 10,000 children in 170 schools have participated. Reframing it as my personal tikkum olam has helped me keep my dancing feet grounded—in a school, in a prison, and even on a Caribbean island.

Chapter 6

Travels with Father

One morning I received a phone call from a Catholic priest.

"I'd like to study dance with you."

"I'm sorry, all I have for beginner adults is a class for older women. We're very raucous; we constantly talk about really inappropriate subjects. It's not a good fit for you."

"I called you. You didn't call me," he said. The next morning at seven AM, a Rob Lowe lookalike in crisp, ironed sweats and t-shirt walked up the aisle of the auditorium, smiling and waving hello.

"Am I in the right place?" he asked.

"You sure as hell are," one of the women said.

The women requested one of their favorites, Diana Ross singing "Love Hangover." I looked at the priest. He nodded his approval. As it turned out, Father was the sexiest dancer in the class. Mouth open, hips circling ecstatically, his style was pure attention-grabbing, uninhibited joy. One woman asked me if he was a male stripper. A student sidled over to me and whispered, "I want that man to be my love hangover! My sperm donor!"

This is how Father joined my women's dance class. I was to find out that he was leading separate lives: serious about the priesthood, committed to God and to social justice, and a connoisseur of great food, music, dance, and art, with dozens of friends and a flourishing social life.

He lived with a handful of his fellow priests at Mount Saint Alphonsus Retreat Center, an opulent castle-like structure with a hundred

81

bedrooms and a dining room that seats 250 people, set on 400 magnificent groomed acres overlooking the Hudson River along what the locals call "Holy Highway" because there are many monasteries located along route 9W.

Father and I became close friends, inseparable for three years. The glue that held us together was passion for social justice, the arts, and a lot of laughs. If a day passed without seeing each other, we'd talk on the phone.

It was odd to find myself, a Jew, with a role to play at Mount Saint Alphonsus. Father added a dance component to the Mount's retreats for the homeless, AIDS sufferers, and local women participating in a Catholic day of prayer.

The retreats were all-day affairs with meal breaks. I was allowed to sit at the table for the "professed," along with priests, nuns, and other dignitaries. My daughter, Elianah, eight years old, joined us for lunch one day beneath an eight-foot-high crucifix complete with bloody rivulets running down Jesus' face. "What a strange looking sculpture," Elianah remarked. "Does anyone here know the story of that?"

"She's a Martian," I hastened to explain.

In the 1990s, AIDS was a death sentence. Ninety percent of the retreat participants in the AIDS retreat were Black; many had been incarcerated. Addicts and homosexuals danced together in the morning, rehearsed in the afternoon, and performed in the chapel on the evening of the final day. A memorial service commemorating past participants who had died was part of the program.

A huge muscle-bound Black man named Melvin, tears drenching his face, a colostomy bag attached to his waist, and neuropathy in his legs (which made his dancing wobbly), spoke. "I think about you every day. Every time the sun comes up, at night when I cry in bed, all the time, I love you." He lit a candle. "This is for the man who died by my hand." Melvin was the first of many murderers I would come to know.

All my preconceived notions of who violent criminals are was challenged in the moment he lit the candle and allowed his authentic self to shine through.

What I now refer to as "my Catholic period" ended when Father invited me to join him on a peace and justice mission to the Caribbean islands of Dominique and St. Lucia.

I brought my daughter Sarah to assist me. At first, we were given a shabby room in the tropical heat with one twin bed, no air conditioning, filled with dust and dirt. I told Father that I could not sleep under those conditions; I would not have the energy for the dance component unless he provided another place for us to stay. Father got us a spare room in the presbytery where the priests lived, a beautiful house with a swimming pool and air-conditioning. That's when the problems began. I didn't know the rules.

I committed an apparently unforgivable faux pas by shushing another priest who was making noise early in the morning. You don't shush a priest, maybe a rabbi, but not a priest!

Looking back, I think Father's two incompatible worlds collided when I moved into the presbytery.

The dance space secured for the workshops was a windowless metal shed. Inside it was twenty degrees hotter. Mist hung in the air like smoke house pea soup. The students, accustomed to the weather, appeared cool and pleasant. I taught an adaptation from the first movement of Alvin Ailey's *Revelations*, "I've Been 'Buked," and an African dance.

The second day, the students arrived carrying mangoes as a gratitude offering. After the workshop, the students walked with me back to the presbytery.

On the islands, I found abundant raw talent, grace, and gratitude. A group of students came to us on the day we left. "We are here to say goodbye to the mister and his daughters. But Miss Susan, no goodbye, she is staying with us." I promised that I would come back not knowing then it would be impossible without the sponsorship of the Catholic Church.

Father and I haven't seen each other in many years, our friendship dissolved after the Caribbean peace and justice mission. My relationship with Father changed the direction of my life forever. Were it not for him, I would never have been to the AIDS retreat where I met Melvin, the former prisoner who prayed for the man he'd killed. And it was Melvin, lighting his candle for the man who had died at his hand, who led me to prison work.

Chapter 7

——— ❧ ———

Losing Hugo

My first youth company dissolved as each dancer left for college. FiguresInFlight 2 began with my daughters, Elianah and Sarah, and the most talented students from the Ellenville residency. I continued to teach classes in downtrodden Ellenville, finding it a rich source of the diversity I sought for the company. Most of the students were poor and could not pay. The parents solicited sponsorship from a few successful business establishments.

Ellenville Lumber Company

Dear Susan,

Shots down Center Street last week; an armed robbery at the Hobo Deli just out of town yesterday, you got to be a little crazy to think dance is part of the solution, I must be a little crazy too, here's three months tuition for Inez.

Irwin

When FiguresInFlight 1 ended, I believed I could never love another group as much, but from the start the new group won my heart. Along with my daughters Elianah and Sarah, there were Jonathan and Jesus Villagas, recently arrived with their single mother from Puerto Rico; Bethany Wootan, the youngest of eleven children; Marcus

Wright; Lindsey Green; Kaitlin Lambert; and Samantha Ellis, all from Ellenville; also Sky Gewant, Laura Newman, Tullah Sutcliffe and Rudy Mathis, from the more affluent communities.

A small mountain range and twenty miles separate New Paltz and Ellenville. The culture gap is much wider; the mountain might as well be a mile high, the towns distant as Kentucky and Katmandu. Some parents smoked pot with their children, others spanked them; one family was devoutly religious. Some were poor, others upper middle class. Some were good students, others struggling. But despite their vast differences in race, culture, economics, religion, and upbringing, these thirteen young people worked together for nine years as if their souls were connected.

No hash-tagging, Facebook, tweeting, YouTube, or Instagram existed then. People had only just begun to screen phone calls; the answering machine was as far as personal communication technology had developed. Shorthand like LOL and YOLO hadn't developed yet. The students spoke in complete sentences. Many dances involved intersex partnering and lifts, which the students handled without self-consciousness.

Each student brought something of value besides dance. Singers, athletes, and musicians added their perspectives and talents. Because of the distance and each family's different rules for socializing, the company members did not get to see each other outside of dance classes and rehearsals as often as they'd have wished. The times they were together had a celebratory feel, hard work mixed with jubilance at being together. Purpose took center stage; if a student fell below the expectation level of the group, that student was reprimanded by the others. Loyalty was to the process and the choreography, not to each other. When I got in the way of the rehearsals and they knew the steps better, they asked me not to interfere. Inwardly I beamed with pride. It seemed that the pedagogy I'd developed enabled them to be mature artists.

No matter how foreign to their own life experience an image or narrative was, they would dance it with uncanny ability. In the dance *West Nile*, we worked with themes of isolation and connection. A memory from my trip to India inspired me to direct them to come out of the wings as if they were beggar children, which they did with authenticity and conviction.

In 1996—before the Columbine school shooting became a high-profile issue in the schools, ushering in a period of intense national soul-searching about bullying, my daughter Rebekah and I collaborated on a dance drama on the subject. The script was fairly mild; we wanted it to reach grades 3-8. In the early version, a child was bullied for shyness. When the Columbine High School massacre occurred in April 1999, we had been touring the play extensively for years in New York schools. Being shy was too benign a reason for bullying after a rash of school shootings, as the shooter was often a victim of bullying.

The play was inherited by the next company, FiguresInFlight 3. The story became vividly real when Devon Yankowski, a discovery from a fourth-grade attention residency in Woodstock, volunteered herself as target. Bullied throughout her school years for being overweight, Devon owned the role as the big girl who triumphs when it is her turn to bully the bully and she chooses the higher road, befriending him instead. Devon could do it all, jump high, turn and express emotions.

Both Devon and her mother Ingrid, who became company administrator, were unapologetically "fat," and not afraid of that word either. They came to rehearsal with bags of chips and nibbled throughout class and rehearsal. Both were angry and good at it, accomplices in finding other people impossibly irritating. When I met Devon and Ingrid, Ingrid had already been diagnosed with cancer. She achieved remission for five years before the cancer returned. She died years later after a ferocious, courageous battle. Her anger had seemed to be a source of her strength.

FiguresInFlight 3 had eleven boys and eight girls. The majority of the boys came from an attention residency at Rosendale Elementary School. Teachers are not supposed to like one student more than the others, but Hugo, a ten-year-old who worked like an adult, was my favorite. Hugo had all the physical talent, flexibility, good feet, high jumps, balanced turns; with all the expressive talent to go with it. He never missed a class or rehearsal. When it wasn't his turn to dance, he practiced on the sidelines.

The Saturday Hugo missed rehearsal was just a little emptier for me. That rainy evening Sarah and I were on our way to Upstate Cinema, a movie house in Rhinebeck, NY, when Hugo called. I joked with him, pretending to berate him for missing rehearsal before he had the chance to speak. He let me finish. Then he told me he was in the hospital diagnosed with leukemia.

The first visit Elianah and I made to Sloan Kettering, a transit strike in New York City meant we had to walk from Port Authority on 41st Street to the hospital on 67th Street. There was a foot of snow on the ground. We were soaked in icy slush up to our knees. I glanced at Elianah trudging though the damp. She looked so strong. I felt guilty. Why was my child healthy, and theirs not?

Seeing Hugo lying so still and small in the bed, using a walker to take a few steps down the hallway for "exercise," was a shock. Elianah sang "Nothing's Going to Harm You" from Sweeney Todd while Hugo gazed up at her rosy, healthy face, her thick shiny black hair catching the light from the hospital window. The dancing boy was gone, replaced by a ghost, a weak boy. For comfort Hugo listened over and over again to the Beatles song "Let It Be." His hair had gone, which he hid under a hat. It was a great source of pain and fear for him to be bald, with its association with frail old age.

Hugo spent six months at Sloan Kettering Hospital. Everyone wrote on his Caring Bridge web page, messages of hope and support.

One Saturday, the dancers created a play with super heroes who killed cancer cells and filmed it and gave it to Hugo.

In spite of losing Hugo, we rehearsed every Saturday from 9 to 3.

Our venue was in the basement of a private school. There were often others in the building on Saturday for one reason or another, so I ignored the sound of steps until they reached the upper landing closest to the staircase. To our joy, amazement, and surprise it was Hugo, looking frail but smiling from beneath his hat, his parents trailing behind. Just released after six months in the hospital, he'd been given the choice of whether to go home or go directly to the dance studio. Hugo chose to reunite with his dance company.

We formed a circle around him.

Jubilant, safe at last among the barres and mirrors and most of all, among his dance family, Hugo flung his hat to the floor exposing his bald head to his peers in an unforgettable gesture of victory and trust. When still only a child, he knew in that group of people he could be his authentic self. We took this as a gesture of gratitude.

A couple of months later Hugo performed for the last time with FiguresInFlight, opening the show with a solo to the gospel classic "Be Grateful" by Walter Hawkins. But Hugo's spirit was stronger than his body. He overworked, became exhausted, and began to miss classes. What had been beautiful curved dancer's feet were weak and flat after months in bed. Savvy about dance, he was aware that he wasn't as good as he had been. After a few more tries, he stopped coming.

Chapter 8

The Dream of Prison Work

Why do some people with rough beginnings find ways to wring beauty from the tears and chaos, while others never recover and carry on the vicious cycle? What drove me to paint and make dances with such obsessive fervor? How did my childhood traumas lead me to make art rather than police blotter headlines?

I've found insight in the work of Alice Miller, a Swiss psychologist of Polish-Jewish origin who did groundbreaking work on parental child abuse. In *The Untouched Key* she explores the clues, often overlooked in biography, that connect childhood traumas to adult creativity. Studying my paintings for clues to myself, I noticed a recurring theme; children in neat beautiful interior settings—just another element in a still life, often surrounded by fruit and flowers; a carefully posed setup, everyone clean and pleasing just like Mother would have wanted. Was I still trying to make it right, fit myself into her image of who she wanted me to be? It's no wonder that movement eventually became my rebellion against the static pictures I created on paper. No, I would not be still. I would dance!

Reading the books of Alice Miller, contemplating the various degrees of rape I had survived three decades earlier, I began to face the results of my childhood circumstances. Without effective love from either parent, I'd been desperate for love and attention. Yet this result certainly hadn't been intentional on their part. It was simply a function of their own limitations.

Dancing had saved me. I believed, hundreds of children later, that it was good medicine for almost anyone. And the dream of teaching dance in prison again came my way.

A Nun on a Bus

Having been tossed out of the Highland DFY for bullying a staff member, I doubted I'd get another chance to teach dance in prison. Still, I tried. I drove past Eastern Correctional Facility in Napanoch, on my way to Ellenville residencies; a huge surreal castle-like structure at the foot of the mountain separating New Paltz from Ellenville. Eastern Correctional has something of a reputation in the New York State Department of Corrections for progressive educational programming. I called and asked if I could come and teach dance.

I was informed that the very idea was ridiculous. "We get all kinds of nuts who want to come in and teach crazy stuff." "People who are just curious. Do-gooders." "Jackasses" was not quite stated, but implied.

I wasn't interested in crime. I wanted to teach men to dance who were not free so they could feel free. The AIDS retreat, the boys in FiguresInFlight, the boys in the school residencies—seeing the way males responded to the powerful, masculine Horton technique, popularized by the Alvin Ailey Company, fueled my desire to bring dance behind the walls. Working with imprisoned boys had confirmed that dance, perhaps especially for men, brings about a powerful emotional outlet. Years later I read about the differences in male and female brains. There were some studies that confirmed men were more adept at expressing emotions nonverbally and women better at talking through their emotions. Yet another indication that dance could be a healing art for incarcerated men. The prison boys were every bit as capable as any suburban child of making the connection between attention and love, more so than some.

It took a nun on a bus to finally get me into the men's prison. Actually, it was a benevolent conspiracy of nuns. I've completely forgotten why I was on the bus that day, but I remember I was sitting up front, not in the mood for company—I'd actually stuck a newspaper on the next seat, hoping people would sit elsewhere, and they did. But when I looked around, it turned out that the elderly nun in the seat behind me was someone I knew.

The man sitting next to her, in a ball cap, was leaning as far away from her as he physically could without jumping out the window. I invited her to join me and we renewed our acquaintance.

We'd met at one of Father's Woman's Day of Prayer events. I'd half-jokingly asked her to tell me the story of her life. She surprised me by complying. She'd entered the convent at sixteen and remained a virgin all her life. When I asked her if she was ever secretly regretful, her eyes got moist. "Sometimes," she said, "I would have liked to be a mother."

"We love the Jews," she also said. "You know, Christ our savior is a Jew." I'd heard that one before, but the temptation to roll my eyes or explain why Jews don't see it as loving to be slain by tens of thousands in Jesus' name melted when I realized that to her this was the nicest compliment she could give me.

Now, on the bus, I told her about being kicked out of the boy's prison. "Oh, my dear!" she said. "What's to become of your prison ministry? I will pray to our Lord to reinstate it."

Jews don't have "ministries;" we don't evangelize, and for the most part, secular Jews don't pray for favors. My reaction to losing the program had been to beat my chest in woe, hang some psychological crepe. This will never happen again, I told myself. It's over. I'd blown it.

"We are a contemplative order," the sister continued. "There are only twelve of us. We're old; some of us used to teach and be out in the world, but now we just pray. Would you come visit us at the convent and tell us about your prison ministry? Then all of us will put you in our daily prayers."

I was not about to let the fact that she kept calling it a ministry prevent me from talking about dance for prisoners. Bearing organic vegetables from my garden and a videotape of the incarcerated boys, I made my way back to Mount Saint Alphonsus, where I'd spent so much time with Father during my "Catholic period."

Eight aging nuns looked at tapes of the boys dancing in their red prison garb to "Amazing Grace" sung by the Harlem Boys Choir, "Someday We'll All Be Free" by Donny Hathaway, and an upbeat Eastern European Jewish klezmer piece that the dancers introduced by reciting Yiddish words with perfect pronunciation; Mel Brooks couldn't have done any better. This unusual component began when I slipped in a yiddishism while teaching. "What's that?" they asked. To which I replied, "My Ebonics." They thought the words were funny and wanted to learn more of "Miss Susan's Ebonics." Silly sounding words made them laugh, and in a prison laughter is a sound that seems to cleanse the atmosphere of negativity.

The nuns listened as Dudley talked about the dance program. "Dance is a learning experience for me, something new. When Miss Susan and Bethany are here the whole place, prison, falls away. And for two hours, it's just about what we're doing, learning the choreography, working together to make something beautiful happen. I forget everything, how much I miss my momma, what it feels like to be locked up. I'm only sixteen; I'm in here for two years. But dancing is great. I feel so much joy!"

On the video I said to Dudley, "You are my student." We looked at each other for a long moment. "And you are my teacher," he said.

94

All the nuns were crying. One was almost hysterical. "Tell someone to let that sweet boy out," she sobbed, sounding like a little girl. "He's a lovely child!"

"Tell us, what is your biggest wish for your prison ministry?"

Well, if they were going to pray...Go big, I thought. I reeled off my most ludicrous fantasy.

"I want to teach grown men in an adult prison, then when they get released I want to continue training them, taking them touring all over the world inside of prisons in every country in the world. After that we'll go to Broadway, have a big hit, make lots of money, and send more people inside to teach other prisoners to dance, until millions of prisoners worldwide are dancing!"

"Someone already did that," said a nun. "Well, maybe not exactly that, it was theater not dance. There is an organization called Rehabilitation Though the Arts, the prisoners, performed for one night on Broadway. The show was called *Sing Sing* on Broadway. The woman's name is Katherine Vockins. Maybe you should get in touch with her."

Katherine Vockins told me politely that modern dance in an adult men's prison would never work. I knew without a doubt she was wrong. We talked, and despite her skepticism, she agreed to travel from her home in Westchester to New Paltz to watch videos of the boys and hear my pitch.

I made a quiche. Between bites I gave her the hard sell, with the nun connection since she was a serious Christian. She was impressed by unexpected brilliance of the dancing, Dudley's comments, and my passion-filled pitch. She left willing to talk to her board members one time and see if they would approve.

"Just let me in once," I said.

The next day I received a letter in the mail from an old friend. I hadn't heard from Ann in years.

Dear Susan,

I was thinking about your work with the boys and I recently came across this article I thought might interest you.

The article was about Katherine Vockins. I stood by the mailbox trying to calculate the odds of receiving this letter that day, about the woman I had met with the day before. I called Katherine and told her the coincidence must have been arranged by God, an argument I thought she'd understand. I told her that in Hebrew the word is *bash-ert*, literally translated as "destiny." It is often used in the context of a divinely foreordained marriage partner, but it can also apply to any God-inspired coming together of energies; which is what happened the day I stepped inside of Woodbourne Correctional Facility.

Chapter 9

⁂

Woodbourne

Woodbourne Correctional Facility was built in 1932 on a property that consisted of 600 acres of prime farmland. In a few places inside of Woodbourne are works of art, placed by skilled architects who were employed by the government through the Works Project Administration. The goal of WPA public building programs was to end the Depression and alleviate its worst consequences. Millions of people needed subsistence incomes. Government-funded work relief was preferred over public assistance because it maintained self-respect, reinforced the work ethic, and kept skills sharp. The artisans who built Woodbourne had a vested interest in extending their employment by adding extra, aesthetically-beautiful details.

In a courtyard in the belly of the prison the artisans who built Woodbourne carved dozens of relief sculptures on imitation Greek columns: man running from a policeman, the scales of justice, mysterious letters and images, all giving a sense of beauty and importance to the building. Topping many of the columns are detailed gargoyles, exquisitely rendered. It is rumored that Woodbourne was designed to suggest a monastery more than a prison. The grandeur of the courtyard is in sharp contrast to the drab impoverished appearance of the town.

The small village of Woodbourne in the Sullivan County Catskills consists of one street of shops. For three-quarters of the year, it's a ghost town. Beginning immediately after Memorial Day, thousands of Hasidic Jews flock from locations all over the world to spend the summer in Woodbourne and neighboring communities like Ellenville, Liberty,

97

and Monticello. Faded Hebrew letters adorn signs in front of all the stores selling Judaica: religious paraphernalia, kosher food, and proper modest clothing for women and girls.

Married women wear long skirts and loose tops, and cover their heads with scarves, turbans or wigs. The children, from very large families, are dressed alike, as were my sister Bunny and I during our childhood.

You can get some real Jewish bagels in Woodbourne in the summertime. I walked into the aromatic bakery one Sunday before going inside the prison, a Jewish woman in pants with my hair hanging naked on my 68-year-old shoulders, signaled to the baker that I was not religious. He knew from my appearance that I might be Jewish. The baker asked me in a thick Yiddish accent what I was doing in Woodbourne.

"Guess," I answered.

Stroking his long grey beard, head cocked sideways, he peered at me through rimless glasses.

"I don't need to guess," he finally declared. "I am going into the back of the store. I will ask God and he will tell me."

Had he returned and said, "God tells me that you are teaching modern dance to the prisoners up on the hill," I would be writing this wearing a long skirt and a wig. Thank God, God told him I was "maybe visiting a relative."

Katherine met me at the gate the first day. I was dressed appropriately, in a FiguresInFlight t-shirt and a pair of loose stretch pants.

The inappropriate item I wore was a big invisible chip on my shoulder. Without any real knowledge of how adult prisons worked, I reverted to my arrogant hippie assumptions about "the man:" the people whose job it is to provide care, custody and control of the prison population. Meanwhile, I was outraged at the idea that they might have preconceived notions about me as a woman volunteer, which they did. The volunteers had a reputation for having unrealistic ideas about the men, loving and only seeing good in them, and being left-wing bleeding-heart liberals, which for the most part we were.

My reeducation took a while. At first it was automatic to lump all the correctional officers together, assuming their politics, level of education, and opinion of the inmates to be as similar as the uniforms they wore and generally—to my liberal gaze—pretty low-grade. I would come to find out that on both sides of the bars and for all the various reasons that people found themselves inside of that vast building on any given day, we were all simply human beings as varied and similar as any group of people anywhere—administrators, officers, prisoners, and volunteers.

There are correctional officers doing their jobs with wisdom and compassion. There are administrators who fight for humanistic and enlightened policy changes. There are volunteers with ulterior motives and prejudices of their own. There are dangerous psychopath predators, too badly damaged to be trusted. And there are prisoners like the men in my program, jewels in the crown of FiguresInFlight 5. But it would be impossible to work effectively in a prison without understanding the stereotypes these groups hold about each other, and between prison volunteers and correctional officers, there are plenty.

Much of the work of correctional officers is boring, offering little satisfaction. They see the volunteers, often educated, some attractive young women, fawning all over the inmates, teaching them lessons that the officers may have to struggle to afford or get for their own children. Some volunteers are openly arrogant and patronizing, coming in with the belief that what they bring is vastly superior to food, shelter, clothing, safety, conflict resolution and the million other necessities the Department of Corrections are called upon to provide.

In the beginning, the officers put me through a special kind of hazing as they escorted me to the assigned classroom on Sundays.

* "There are a lot of sex offenders here who don't care how old you are or if you're the ugliest or oldest woman alive!" they would say, reaching for the most terrifying thing about which they could think.

* "They're animals; you can be sure they look at you like any other female that comes in here."

* "These men are con artists. They act one way when you're around, but you can't trust them."

* "Why are you wasting your time? Why don't you work with victims?"

* "Dance? That's crazy, as soon as they get out they will never dance again. Off come the crosses, the Muslim caps… it's all phony. It's that young girl you bring with you. They just want to gawk at a female."

* "I got to be friends with one of them. He left and came back, I asked him why, and it turned out he robbed a family at gunpoint. He forgot to mention that after the robbery he raped their ten-year-old daughter. I never spoke with him again."

There was another side to the officers, these men who spent their working lives inside the fences. As I became a familiar face, I started to hear other things too. One Sunday night a correction officer, while escorting me through the building down to the room where I taught dance, asked me if I was Jewish. When I told him, he said he was Jewish too, but I would not approve since he was a Jew for Jesus. Then he said, "God has put me in this prison to do his work. I see hundreds of men a day, I treat them with respect. Every man I see I pray for and secretly bless. There but for the grace of God go I. I could have been locked in here just as easily."

The magical thought occurred to me that maybe he wasn't real, that he was an angel. It was the strangest encounter with an officer that I ever had. I never saw him again.

Over time, officers sometimes spoke words of empathy.

* "A lot of these guys wouldn't be here, maybe most, if they'd had the money for proper representation."
* "If you treat them with respect, they treat you with respect. I try to treat them well, it's not my job to punish them. Being locked up is punishment enough."

My favorite:

* "I couldn't tell this to anyone else but you. I can't stand the men I work with. I much prefer the inmates."

The first day, the officer in the lobby asked me to sign a guest book and give him my car keys. I was instructed to walk through a metal detector, which I set off. I took off my shoes, tried again, and again lights buzzed on, an alarm sounded. A hand-held wand was waved up and down my body, several times, until the culprit was determined to be my underwire bra. I was told not to wear that again or I would have to remove it, have it examined by an officer before I could go into the facility. My hand was stamped with an image only visible under a black light.

The officer took us up a few steps into a small foyer. A loud clanging gate shut behind us. I stuck my hand through a narrow opening; black light shone from inside the slot, and I heard an officer I could not see yell "Okay!" from behind the two-way mirror. Thick horizontal bars in front of the mirror protected the officer from any potential aggression. I looked into the mirror and saw an image of myself behind the bars.

We entered a long corridor that led to a room in the belly of the prison. Waiting for us were twenty men. Most were Black or Hispanic, "people of color," as prison dancer David Navarro would years later teach me was the proper term.

Just as the boys had been, the men were impeccably groomed and pressed, hair in braids or dreads or neatly cropped. They were in "state greens," polyester pants issued by the prison. Many had wrist watches, some expensive-looking. Their shoes appeared new and very clean, white sneakers without a smudge of dirt. I would come to find out these were cleaned nightly with toothpaste and toothbrush.

These men were like the boys, only older. They had powerful precision bullshit detectors and I knew I had to be real. "My name is Susan Slotnick. When I was a little girl I was very unhappy. I felt trapped. I didn't belong in the family and community where I grew up, so I would dance the sad away. Then I was free, relaxed. Dancing gave me the strength to endure my circumstances. I know that doesn't even come close to your circumstances, but I wondered one day, where do people need to feel free who aren't free? A prison popped into my head.

"For five years I volunteered teaching dance at the Division for Youth prison in Highland. (Invariably, at least one man would raise his hand and tell me he'd been locked up there as a child.) I enjoyed it so much and it was very successful. For me it became the most fulfilling teaching experience of my career until I was kicked out."

Then I told the story about strong-arming an official into changing a light bulb, which I told very charmingly, and it got a laugh. I went on to tell of the nun on the bus and all that followed.

"I'm not here to do a good deed or save anyone. I hope to replicate the experience I had with the boys. If you are willing and you like the program, I'll come back every Sunday. And besides dance, I teach a philosophy loosely based in the work of Gurdjieff, a mystic whose ideas are popular in certain esoteric communities all over the world. It is about the magic of attention. I am going to tell you about it right now and afterwards we will practice the concept as we learn some dance moves."

"Attention is the main ingredient in love. One cannot care for anything without first directing attention to it. But all of you know this already. How many of you played on monkey bars when you were a kid?" My daughter Rebekah, who teaches dance and drama in Queens, told me just about every child in the inner city could relate to that image. I taught the same material I did in the residencies; it worked just as well.

"What did you say to your parent or whoever was taking care of you every time you pulled yourself across the bars, did a trick? No matter how many times, dozens, hundreds, you always gave the same command."

"Look at me!" somebody spoke up.

"But why did you want them to look at you? Logically, even a small child knows they've already watched you many times."

"I didn't get much attention growing up. My dad was gone, mom worked a lot, and I had lots of siblings. I said 'look at me' every time. Yes, if they watched me it felt like love."

Years later a formerly incarcerated man would say, in an interview, "Susan taught us that attention equals love. After I really got it, I started to pay attention to myself in a new way. I paid love to myself, and everything in prison changed for me."

After 250 Sundays in the boys' prison, I knew these dancers too. Just like the boys, these men caught on right away. Every time a new group of dancers joins the program—at this writing dozens of times—I have given that same introductory talk.

What was their first impression of me, the material, and dance? I asked dancer Andre.

The first time I saw you, you were like a gypsy woman; the way you were talking was unlike any other volunteer I came across during my incarceration. The whole vernacular was more humane. The attention philosophy right away went deeply into me. You didn't talk down to us. The mentality in other volunteers was often trying to 'save' us, so we kept them at arm's length. We knew no one saves us except ourselves. We didn't want that attitude from the volunteers.

You gave us tools, paying attention, we used them. When you told us what you were about, your intentions, you worked with us, not for us. But honestly, it wasn't you who got me into the dance program, it was dance.

The first performance I saw in the gym, when they danced the piece 'Each Other,' about the violence that brought us here, done so beautifully, was mind boggling. Seeing what the men were doing, I thought, these guys have the guts to do this! I didn't know if I could be a part of it, expose myself to population. I respected the dancers for putting themselves out there, not knowing if they would be heckled or congratulated. That amazed me!

A staff member, a Black guy too—he was my guidance counselor—made the comment after the performance that 'watching this was a waste of my time.' I thought, are you kidding me? This is phenomenal, it's history being made in this prison. I can't believe what I'm seeing. I actually felt bad for him that he couldn't get it.

Right after the show, I went up to my best friend Naquan, one of the dancers. I asked him how do I join? Who should I speak to? When can I start? It was that piece, 'Each Other,' that changed the course of my life in prison and since I got out.

When Zorro Hartford, a recreation teacher at DFY, first told me to check out recording artist Kem's song "Each Other," I ignored him. Over the years, lots of people suggested music after seeing my work, usually not to my taste. Zorro persisted. For weeks he asked me if I had listened. Finally, he made me a CD and I promised to tell him the following Sunday if I would create a dance to it. Right away I knew I'd found a piece of music I would choreograph to as many times, and I have.

The instrumentals are soft, tender, simple and sad. Kem's lyric is a heartfelt plea to God for help as we strive to be human together. I found out that Kem was writing from experience: He'd faced homelessness, addiction, and isolation from his family. He did not overcome these issues until he turned to spirituality and music.

I was awestruck by his song. Could I do it justice? Was I good enough?

Each Other

The men come out one at a time, as if searching for something. One dancer's inner image was that he was searching for himself.

They plant their feet with intention, as if they are stepping into peanut butter. The use of their arms, movement of their backs and carefully placed feet gives the entire dance a catlike, stalking, graceful quality.

In slow motion, violence and mayhem erupt, but the movement remains beautifully executed. A man is punched and falls. Another is stabbed. There is an arrest. An evil man mills around glaring, gleeful, mischievously enjoying watching the cruelty. He is Society.

Two bodies lie on the stage. One is dead, the other hurt. Six men carry the corpse over their heads, pall-bearer style, stepping in slow, solemn unison.

Alone on stage, Society dances, showing a softer side of his nature. He is joined by the other dancers who approach the injured with the same hideous cruelty and curiosity, depicted grotesquely in facial expressions.

On the lyric, "Trying to take a stand for peace," the faces slowly morph into reverential, prayerful beauty. At the words "send us your love," all the dancers pick the injured man up, lift him high, his arms outstretched in a pose of crucifixion. Choreography is subliminal, and in the moment a dance is made the imagery is often unconscious. I didn't realize the audience would see Christ on the cross until a prisoner from the audience told me. I'd had no such intention, but it was "Each Other" that gave me Andre, who would become a key player in my life.

The dance ends with the men in a clump, Alvin Ailey-style, gesturing in perfect unison.

Chapter 10

―――――― ⌗ ――――――

The Rules

After I brought in a video of FiguresinFlight 4, my current outside dance company, they named their dance company FiguresInFlight 5. After a few months, they stopped showering me with repeated, profuse expressions of gratitude after each session and started schooling me in the hopes of reining in some of my outrageous behavior. They did not want me to bring attention to myself. They wanted me to stay.

I was always a rule-breaker, and the vestiges of the rebellious teenaged me found ample targets in the dense prison bureaucracy.

Rule one: No touching.

Impossible. Every dance teacher moves bodies around while illustrating proper placement.

Rule two: Don't give them any personal information.

Impossible. I often used examples from my own life to make philosophical points. If I was honest and willing to share it encouraged them to be vulnerable and honest too, without doing so myself would have put them right back down where I didn't want them, into a relationship of lesser power. Andre and the others trusted me and did not keep me at arm's length because I did not keep them at arm's length.

Rule three: Don't do any favors for them, make no contact with their families.

Impossible. When a prisoner whose mother was dying could not get in touch with his relatives, he asked me to telephone his sister and tell her when he'd have access to a phone.

I called his sister and was told the mother had died that morning. It was not my place to tell him. Not the prison rule but respect for his privacy and a reluctance to intrude on family situations gave me the discipline to teach the class that day without letting him know. It was not easy, but I did it.

Rule four: When explaining a dance exercise, avoid explicit sexual references.

I came up with this one myself. Had the prison establishment had to even think about it, I'd have been out of there. With my freewheeling sixties mentality, there were times I had to remind myself to keep in check. Sometimes things just came out before I realized what I was saying. Like the time the men were in a wide second position plié, stretching, and I told them to "drop your crotch into the floor as if it weighs a ton." That got a gale of guffaws.

Rule five: Don't speak publicly or write about the prison, the men, the policies, or your personal experience inside.

In the newspaper column I write for the local paper I have broken this rule many times. I got around it by not mentioning anyone's name, or the location of the prison. Often, in the small town where I live, I would be stopped in the grocery store, by a stranger who read about the prison and was full of positive responses. Interest in mass incarceration was just beginning to peak in America. I would like to think that my bending of the rule contributed to bringing the plight of prisoners into the foreground.

Once this book is published, I will never be allowed to teach in a prison again. But the cat's out of the bag already. I could be banned tomorrow. If I have to choose between teaching or publishing, it's a no-brainer. I choose teaching.

Rule six: Don't let them give you anything to bring out of the prison.

Impossible. Every birthday, every Mother's Day, when my brother died, they'd spent precious commissary money, hiring a prisoner who had a booming cottage industry inside making elaborate pop-up greeting cards. When my brother died I received these handwritten messages:

"May all the strength and blessing be yours in this time. From the depth of my being wishing you the love and family you need. You can find it from us."

On Mother's Day:

> SISTA Susan, Love is a dance her heart the beat, supreme rhythm or blues feeling you in your feet; knowing and wise in the ways of the world, the beat of a woman but always the rhythm of a girl. May the creator bless you! Happy Mother's Day.

* * *

> You are a gem in a mountain full of rocks. Thank you for being my friend and soul mate. Keep up your God work in the humanity sphere. I have crazy love for you, happy Mother's Day, sweetie.

* * *

> Thank you for allowing me to become someone I never dreamed I could be. Dance makes me feel innocent again. You did that

and although I could never forgive myself for what I have done, your class helps me live with it.

* * *

Did you ever imagine that you would have so many sons? Your heart must be the size of Canada to be able to love us all so much. It's an honor to witness the power of your love.

* * *

Not enough space on this card to express feelings towards you. Thank you for being you and letting us be us.

I saved all the cards. I still have all but one. For my sixty-eighth birthday the men commissioned a pop-up card, which opened two arms jutted forward with the caption, "Here's a birthday hug." When the prison officials saw the card, they disallowed it under the pretext that it was inappropriate and suggested physical contact. The hug was coming from a piece of paper!

Rule seven: Intimate expressions of love between volunteers and prisoners are strictly forbidden.

Impossible. All the volunteers grew to love the men. That did not mean anything untoward would happen. Like well-blended dough that must rise, all the conditions are ripe for love to grow; making art, being authentic, sharing stories, with massive amounts of gratitude coming from both sides made love inevitable. Older female volunteers became much-needed surrogate mothers. I was scolded by some of the dancers for loving them so much it bordered on babying, since I felt so maternal towards them.

Every year all volunteers sign an agreement with the Department of Corrections stating we will not have sex with prisoners. Breaching the agreement is a crime akin to having sexual contact with a child, because prisoners have no legal right to consent.

You did hear of the occasional serious romance, in which a volunteer forfeited her status in exchange for visits with her man, in the hope of a prison wedding.

The waves of love that crash over an effective volunteer in prison are ubiquitous. I have spoken with many volunteers; the response is the same. They love the men, the laughter, the making art, the belief that what we are doing really matters.

I tried to start another dance program in another prison. It was a disaster that nearly cost me everything.

Eastern Correctional Facility, that first prison I called years before, is a maximum-security prison, twenty miles away from Woodbourne, about ninety miles north of New York City. I still passed it on my way to teach. Around a bend, heading into the hamlet of Napanoch, there's a large cornfield to the east. Looming above the trees, at the far edge of the field against the background of the Shawangunk Mountains, is an extraordinary castle-like structure with a pyramid-style green roof, fortified by battlements and cone-capped turrets. It's a surreal, shockingly beautiful building housing over a thousand prisoners, sometimes nicknamed "Happy Nappy" for its beautiful setting, relative peace, and the fact that New York City relatives can get there to visit in under two hours.

A popular, dedicated volunteer teacher, much loved by the men, had just been booted out. This teacher came from a distance to teach theater and mount productions. When her class was cancelled, she was not always told. Once she'd arrived in a snow storm, only to turn around and drive a long way home in a blizzard.

Supposedly, a prisoner called her from a contraband phone one day to tell her the theater class was cancelled. The possession of a cell phone is taken as seriously as a weapon inside a prison. It was rumored that this prisoner had a phone, or (depending on who was telling the story) that he had found a way to use the phone at his work site within the prison industries. Either way, it was the assumption that she had given him her number. After that, she was thrown out of teaching in any New York prison.

If one has access to a phone, one has access to directory assistance too. He could easily have found her phone number on his own. But prison policies and decisions were often illogical. She had no recourse; it was over.

I showed up on the heels of that beloved theater teacher's dismissal, and was given the same students. I suppose the authorities thought dance was an apt replacement for theatre. Not so the men, who believed I was sent by the administration to gauge the mood of the angry, disappointed students. I knew nothing about this, but the vibes were odd.

My first day, I was escorted by Vinnie, an old man in his 90s. He was a World War II veteran who still wore his combat medals on his prison uniform jacket. He crept along at a funereal pace, and all the while he talked about World War II. Eastern has an enormous auditorium with a presidium stage, and only the stage is lit. The dark made me uncomfortable. Unlike at Woodbourne, there was no correctional officer present in my line of sight.

Immediately I sensed something was wrong. The men looked at me with distrust and suspicion. I went into my spiel but for the first time ever the words seemed to vanish into the darkness, echoing back without a response. What I did not find out until later was that for the second time in my life I was suspected of being a spy. Just like with my Gurdjieff group, it took several sessions before the others began to trust me.

During this time, which was just before the Rockefeller laws were finally repealed—allowing thousands of men to return home—one man in the Eastern program told me his story. He got thirty years to life for a drug charge. I apologized to him.

"I've been here since 1978 and no one has ever apologized to me. Thank you," he said.

One day I arrived at Eastern with a greater than usual feeling of trepidation. Vinnie seemed deteriorated, although that did not stop him from talking non-stop all the way to the auditorium. His slow steps and fast talk made me squirm with impatience, patience being a virtue I do not possess.

There were only two men who showed up in the huge auditorium. The boom box was locked in a closet, and no one had the key. With no music, and only two students, an inner whisper told me I should just leave, but one of the men was a fine surrealist painter. He had a scrapbook of pictures to show me. We talked for two hours about art. I forgot where I was. Standing up to leave, I felt unsafe relying on Vinnie for protection. Without thinking I clasped the young painter's arm while I was escorted down the hallway leading to the gate. We passed many prisoners and officers without comment.

Suddenly I heard a loud voice scream "Halt!" The young painter was grabbed by two officers and put in a cage the size of a very small closet. In robotic tones, another officer told me to follow him. For the next two hours, I was interrogated about "the incident."

Why didn't I leave when I could not teach? What were we talking about all that time? What was he showing me? Didn't I know all touching was forbidden? Did I have a special relationship with him?

I got a taste, a bitter one, of what it must be like to be a prisoner.

The authorities wrote up a report calling my clasping his arm in public an "embrace." As with the theater teacher, I was told, I would probably lose my volunteer status forever.

I left the prison in misery coupled with fear, sure that I had lost everything. But instead of making a right turn to go home, I made a snap decision and turned left to Woodbourne. I needed immediate advice from Jean King, the deputy of programming at Woodbourne. That decision not only saved me, but was the beginning of an important friendship. Deputy King and I worked side-by-side making the dance program a success. She was an anomaly among prison administrators, with unwavering concern for the 800 men in her care.

A good programming director is a very busy person. It was sheer luck that I found Jean in her office. She's a woman with a no-nonsense personality, the type who should be running the entire system: troubleshooting, listening to upset people, and solving problems are her strength, specialty, talent and skill.

Jean doesn't wear compassion on her sleeve, she's tough but fair and doesn't mince words when it comes to telling the truth. She told me to calm down. Like a command from a stern but composed mother, the injunction to chill out quieted my inner turmoil. Step by step, she told me what would happen. She believed it would be possible for me to continue at Woodbourne for the time being, at least until the matter was settled.

I was told by an Eastern administrator to call a man who would review my case and decide my fate. I was advised to be prepared for laborious, lengthy phone conversations. Patience would be needed.

After many calls in which I was asked the same questions over and over, and much time spent listening to the loquacious gentleman, he finally called me with the outcome.

"You will never be allowed into Eastern Correctional again, but you will be able to continue at Woodbourne."

He offered to tell me how he'd arrived at his decision. "I told my wife about you taking that fellow's arm and she said 'That woman sounds like a very compassionate person. Let her be.' My wife is my life and she is as wise as a judge in the Bible. I always listen to her opinion."

I was let back inside. Outside, I was still conducting dance residencies, painting, writing for the local newspaper, directing and choreographing FiguresInFlight 4, which was off to a rocky start.

Chapter 11

Love Happens

I hadn't wanted to start a fourth dance company. Each group lasted about thirteen years and involved an intense emotional investment in a dozen or more students and their families. I taught at least ten thousand classes, and thousands more counting rehearsals with FiguresInFlight 1, 2, and 3 by the time they left for college. I dealt with parents, money, rehearsal space, venues, scheduling, and finding performance opportunities, which was often a hard sell with youth companies. I directed the summer camp, during which the teachers lived with us. Whether the teachers were a joy or a nightmare all of them wanted my attention after the grueling day of summer dance camp, twenty-four summers in a row.

At first, FIF4 was not interesting to me, all girls but for one boy, all White, most from the same private school and family cultures. They were privileged, similar in body type, very pretty, skinny girls except for two, mostly looking like teen models. I wondered if technology didn't play a role in the lack of emotional connection to the dances, to me, and outwardly to each other. This was the first group who'd grown up with internet access, cell phones, social media, and texting. They didn't listen to each other. In the dance studio, their communication seemed like status updates or tweets, randomly tossed into the air, without a response. When I tried to teach philosophy, especially when illustrating a point with a personal story, their faces remained blank. Rarely did they ask a question. After the swift and intense connections I was used to making, it was strange.

One seventeen-year-old student did ask me why I'd had Rebekah and Sarah fifteen years apart. I decided, as I often do, to tell her the simple truth:

"My best friend committed suicide, and I didn't menstruate for a decade. Then I went on a water fast for twenty-one days, read spiritual books and prayed, after which I got pregnant with Sarah." I was curious to see if such a terse, shocking personal answer would elicit at least some reaction. The young woman nodded, picked up her backpack, and walked out.

They didn't like me either, and I couldn't really blame them. I didn't hide my frustration. "You used to tell us that we weren't interesting people, just rich privileged White girls from private schools who hadn't experienced hardships," Gwendolyn remembers. "You said we were not like the other groups. You told us our dancing lacked emotional expression and was boring. A lot of us felt that even though we weren't starving Black kids in Africa, we still knew what it felt like to be hungry. You negated our experiences. We didn't need you as much as the other dancers who came before us.

"We stayed because we always knew deep down that you were just trying to evoke better dancing from us. You cared about us. I had gone to dance classes before I came here where the teacher didn't pay attention and would say 'good job' without even looking at us. You didn't say we were doing well when we weren't—that was an indication to me that you were paying attention."

I'd thought they weren't listening. Even through the barriers of my frustration and their video screens, something about attention and love had been getting through.

In the previous companies, I'd had children who failed in school, had emotional problems, depression and panic disorders. There was lots of family drama, divorces and love affairs. One boy's father was in prison. A mother abandoned her family and ran off to Belize with the owner of the local Chinese restaurant.

Whatever struggles the FIF4 dancers endured didn't show on the surface. These were the popular, accomplished, good-looking, 'normal' kids my mother would have wished for, the ones who would never have been friends with the likes of me.

Also, I was sixty when they began at the age of five. My right knee was damaged from demonstrating exercises and steps only with my right leg. It was difficult to walk up stairs. Demonstrating dance exercises for thirty-five years only on the right was stupid, and now I was paying the price. Every few months the list of what I couldn't do lengthened; no more jumps, no more full pliés in first position, then in second, no more flatbacks, no more laterals.

How was I to teach combinations without executing any of the movements? Summer program, which had always been my chance to dance for me, was finished. I watched the beautiful younglings dance from a chair. Once in a while I'd get up and try to do a minimal amount of moving, only to sit down. A sixty-year-old trying to keep up with a sixteen-year-old was a sad and ludicrous thing.

I was used to being loved; in the prison, at the residencies, with my daughters, with my husband, and with the members of my former companies. Not knowing if the students liked me took some of the spontaneity out of my teaching style. For the first time, when a lesson fell on flat ears, I was self-conscious, which further interfered with my enjoyment. Did I appear to be just some eccentric, crazy old lady? If that's the way they perceived me, I gave them plenty of material.

"I was eleven when I began dancing with you. My most vivid memory is you continually calling yourself a bitch, then covering your mouth and apologizing," recalls Liam Appelson. "I thought 'bitch' was a really cool word. You got flustered, but you didn't stop!" This was perfect proof that I was afraid I was being too hard on them.

I kept forgetting that they were children. When they were five, I choreographed a dance when they suddenly fell to the floor. "Here's where you get to die," I commanded. They'd just drop in a heap laughing. They were fun then, as they got to be pre-adolescent they became more reserved in class.

An improvisation: "You are blind. Pretend your arms are also legs. Now, suddenly you can see. Scurry along on all fours looking at each other, reacting differently to each person." They did their best to comply, outrageous as the demands must have seemed.

In spite of the problems, in high school they became good dancers and surpassed my other companies in technical proficiency. I began to create dances with serious themes. We were accepted into the prestigious Battery Dance Festival for three consecutive summers.

For the first time—and the last—my dances were reviewed.

New York Times:

> The 19 children who performed in three pieces choreographed by Susan Slotnick for her FiguresInFlight Dance Company (from upstate New York) included only one boy, Liam Appelson. While he was almost its smallest member, he was also perhaps its best, precisely showing the accentuation of each step and, at the end of each work, taking a flying jump off the raised stage with infectious enthusiasm.

This from *iDance Today*, a social network site for dancers.

> FiguresInFlight Dance Company, a young performers dance group, performs three consecutive pieces in the style of contemporary modern dance—*War/Peace On Earth, Unexpected Moments,* and *Stranger in Moscow.* The preteens impress me with their ability to focus on such serious subject matter—they

seem truly eager to present the work—but the pretentiousness of the work is a little off-putting on such fresh little youngsters. With technique, class, and age, they may actually grow into the work they present.

Slotnick's intention for the company—to promote peace in schools and youth—is commendable. If only the style and tone were a touch more relatable, the message might shine brighter, remembering that kids these days are busy texting and usually just waiting for the next bell to ring. Susan Slotnick brags about the students' ability to pull off modern pieces conceptualized for adults, despite being no older than your average Hannah Montana fan.

From an online dance publication:

There were only two outstanding choreographic discoveries at the festival this year. Susan Slotnick presented a sculptural, po-ly-rhythmic musing for a large ensemble, relying on intuitive motions, captured in freeze fame and continuing with cinematic variations.

LOVE HAPPENS

I'd first met Bethany Wootan as a member of FIF2. She was the eleventh and youngest child of a beloved local doctor, and distinguished herself for her talent and her tendency to cry at the slightest provocation. All it took was a story, a song, a heartfelt word and then the tears came. When she cried, the depth of pain and anguish emanating from her little body embarrassed her, which made her weep even more. Her desolation scared all of us, so I would compliment her to ease the discomfort. "Isn't it wonderful how in touch Bethany is with her feelings! We should all be like that."

Sometimes Bethany would call from school, miserable, asking me to pick her up. I would invent a reason, like a doctor's appointment, since misery was not an excuse to be freed from school. She reminded me of myself at that age. She was, as I had been, a creature of secret, passionate interests and lousy grades. As Bethany grew up, she became my apprentice, assisting at residencies and in the DFY, and rehearsal-directing FIF4.

As each student graduated from FiguresInFlight, I made them a goodbye CD of repurposed schmaltzy, inspirational music and pushed them out of the nest. I didn't want my students to get stuck in my orbit. But Bethany had no plans and no place to go. Her father, a general practitioner, was alleged to have taken risks delivering babies at his patients' homes which resulted in his losing his medical license. When she was eighteen her parents sold the family home.

Bethany waited on tables in a local restaurant, living in a rundown apartment with several roommates. She had no plan to go back to school. Every Sunday, including Christmas, she accompanied me to the DFY and later for eight years to Woodbourne. There was something old-fashioned about her ability to be mentored, a graceful quality of patience.

Young, beautiful, kind, and understated, with a Snow White air of purity, all the men at Woodbourne were in love with her. She handled the situation with circumspect dignity, even on the one occasion when the birthday card she received crossed the line between birthday greetings and romance. There was one man with whom she had a special connection, nevertheless she worked through it, on her own, and never allowed her feelings to interfere with our work. During the first several years, Bethany rarely spoke during wrap-up discussions at the end of class.

Only once did Bethany dance in a performance with the men. I choreographed a dance to "With You I'm Born Again," a romantic duet sung by Billy Preston and Syreeta Williams, a heartbreaking and sensual song. The dance begins with three men in chairs using their hands in pantomime, creating the walls of a small prison cell. Bethany dances upstage with her back to the audience, a tactic to keep the prisoners we did not know from seeing too much of her body.

The song is a lover's tender plea for his woman to bring her comfort and sweetness, that he may lie in her arms and be reborn. The choreography, a dance we called *Longing*, ended with Bethany dancing into the same space as the men, choosing one, and innocently, gently clasping hands.

Although Bethany dancing in front of the general prison population was not considered a breach of security and ethics, holding hands was: At the last minute, we changed the step to merely suggest touching. If anything, it added poignancy.

The men in the theater program wrote and performed monologues to introduce each piece. Before *Longing*, a man nicknamed Intelligence Allah recited what he had written.

This potent desire transcends the limitations of vernacular; etched into my heart in each nucleus of my neural network. Call it an inherent hunger having a linguistic home somewhere between yearnings and famished. Born from the cuffs that clenched my wrists when I inherited this in 1994, before the door of a cop car slammed, steering me down the road to a life of loneliness, this inherited hunger, the pains kick in as I rise at sunrise, then consume me at night when I am out of sight of peers. I fight my fears in the solitude of cell bars and concrete walls that demand introspection. In bed I lie, the ceiling becoming a mirror clearer in my eyes, reflecting a truth I acknowledge yet despise, the reality that my forlorn journey in jail is mine to make, the fruit of my labor as a bad apple in a shady bunch.

My views were myopic, molded by five and a half square miles in East NY Brooklyn. My hunger pains are products of misguided ambitions and lost logic; the mindset that placed me in prison, exiled me from my natural counterpart.

This inherent hunger can only be satisfied by a taste of love or its precursor, a woman.

Within this vast sea of testosterone-fueled felons just a drop of sensitivity could quench my thirst; a mere whiff of her scent could save my soul, supply energy to nourish me infinitely propelling me through the remaining three years of my sentence without leaving a carbon footprint. If only I had the blessing of her intuition to add my navigation through the perils of prison. Her presence in the lives of the incarcerated is therapeutic. A smile could silence a cell block, bring boisterous bad boys in Attica to a hush, her touch alleviates stress that permeates within concrete walls with guard towers. Her humanity counters the chaos of incarceration, the inhumane nature of 6-by-9 cells in twenty-three-hour solitary confinement. She is the missing link to the rehabilitative process. I would settle selfishly for her warm embrace if only it was sold in commissary.

A supersized hug would be my ultimate happy meal. I'd order me five each day, one to calm me when I awake with pleasant dreams of her, only to come into the harsh reality of cell bars and gated windows.

Another hug to comfort me after my daily pat frisk by an officer who has a grudge against me because I dare stare inside his eyes instead of bowing in an appeal to authority.

The third hug is to quell my fears of the life-threatening cancer clouds that drift towards me from the swarm of nearby smokers invading my soul as I phone home to family and friends.

The fourth hug is for my fix, yes I confess to being a love junkie. No AA meeting can alter my thinking or the addiction I find divine and so proudly claim to the world is mine. The last embrace is an all-purpose hug, a sympathetic gesture to thwart the reoccurring memories of me, handcuffed shackled watching my father on a hospice deathbed.

Or perhaps a hug to break up the overwhelming monotony of masculinity, the lack of sensitivity void of empathy, taunting me everywhere I go, cellblock, gym, library, grammar class, yard, mess hall at meal, if only I could hear the sound of high heels, light pitched chatter, light hearted laughter. This inherent hunger, doctors can't diagnose it, technology has yet to produce a tool that can detect it, yet the psychological aching feels like internal bleeding from my broken heart. I often awake at night sweating profusely, jaded, gasping for air, overwhelmed by heaving breathing, pondering will the debilitating effects of hunger pains, destroy me, will I die of starvation?

Andre had emerged as a leader in the dance program. He was articulate, fair-minded and able to confront me and the other men when needed, not afraid to express an idea or an emotion. When Andre spoke, we all listened.

I once showed a friend a videotaped interview with Andre. She was stunned. "What's a person like this doing in jail?" I've encountered that attitude many times. Most people on the outside would be surprised at the high quality of some of the people in our jails.

Andre was born in Georgetown, Guyana. When he was one year old his parents immigrated to New York, leaving him with his grandmother, the love of his life. His good looks and natural charm endeared him to his family and neighborhood. Excelling in school and music and dance made his early childhood happy. Georgetown was a wonderful place to be a child: mangoes that fell from trees, music playing all the time, and the freedom to roam safely in crime-free streets.

When he was nine years old, two complete strangers—his parents—showed up and took him to New York City. At first, he was excited. When the reality hit that he was leaving his grandmother and his culture, maybe forever, he was overwhelmed with dread. In the airport, he says he already knew it was wrong for him to come to America. He arrived to find out that his parents were divorced, and his father had remarried. He had half siblings, and would live with his mother.

No matter how hard they both tried, the bond didn't take between mother and son. He missed his grandmother and his home. Alienated, lonely, and sad, he started down the path that so many inner-city kids take, finding a family in the streets. His peers smoked cigarettes, drank beer and skipped school for "hooky jams," midday parties with dancing and music, or just to hang out on the streets smoking weed.

He quit high school, a decision many prisoners have told me sealed their fate and sped their downward spiral into crime. At seventeen, on his way home from committing a robbery with his friends, he became curious about whether he could pull off a robbery by himself. Instead of making a right turn towards his home, he turned left and found another house to rob. That decision, to go right or left, would impact his life forever. He was found sleeping in the house he invaded, convicted, and sent to prison, where he stayed for the next thirteen years.

He estimates it took him nine years to "calm down" and begin to reclaim his childhood self. This is how it happened.

It was three years into my bid. Summer in Lakeview correctional prison, hot, sticky, stale air compounded by being in solitary confinement, locked up 23 hours a day in a tight cell with one window the size of a square foot, if that. It opened like a shade, bars running vertical and wire mesh grid with holes big enough for knats [sic] and mosquitoes to fly through. Summertime in caged up! I tried to sleep on a twin size green plastic covered mattress, the thickness about an inch and a half. The plastic stuck to my skin. In the humid temperature, I sweated so bad on that plastic it was all I could do to not slide off the mattress altogether. The bugs were attracted to a small fluorescent light located above the sink and the toilet bowl. Basically, I was locked up with a cellmate 23 hours a day in a bathroom without ventilation. On one particular night, maybe hotter than usual, I tossed and turned, drenched in my own sweat while knats circled around my head, buzzing. I asked my cellmate to turn off the light but he refused. 'I'm reading I need the light' he said. We went back and forth arguing about the light. The heat, bugs, smells, discomforts, and the reality we were two powerless caged grown men with no control over our lives all adding to our escalating rage. It got ugly and heated. Both of us got out of bed and faced each other with blood in our eyes. I had seen and heard fights happen between cellmates in solitary and it was potentially lethal with dire consequences, even death, always an extended time in prison and in solitary. I admit I was scared.

'Hey man, do we really want to be doing this' I heard myself say followed by some nervous laughter. Something profound, mysterious, a moment of grace, is all I can say to describe what happened next! The blood in our eyes cooled and we found ourselves in a mutual spontaneous hug. Both of us laughed.

My life was permanently changed. After that all anger was gone. I got myself, my life back. Me and my cellmate became brothers. He even tried to fix me up with his sister! Amazing grace, that's what it was. An energy, something besides bugs flew into our cell that night, and caused a change, from deep within me, and I haven't been angry since. Yes, Amazing grace, I will never forget it.

After that he finished high school, went to college, and eventually found his way back to music and dance. By the time Bethany and I met him he was a polite, charming and respectful man with abundant talent. When we performed Longing, he had been in the dance program for several years.

Andre was the first of the dancers to be released. We made dinner plans in Manhattan, my homecoming gift. He never had eaten sushi and was eager to try it. I was expecting to find him sitting in the restaurant waiting for us, but we caught sight of each other on the street. A strange staccato animal yelp escaped my throat. Andre in street clothes, strolling down a sunny New York sidewalk! Free!

The first indication that our relationship would be different was that he never thanked me for the dinner. I was so used to the men inside being ingratiating. It wasn't that he wasn't appreciative and gracious about how much he enjoyed the meal. It was just that his role had shifted. Bethany and my daughters didn't always thank me when I bought them dinner. Andre acted like a member of the family.

Since before Andre's release, we had talked about reworking *Longing* to create a duet for Andre and Bethany. My motive in redoing the dance was to celebrate his freedom to meet a woman, fall in love, and get married—to whomever. I did not have a Machiavellian match-making plan in mind. It would make a moving addition to the coming concert and give the audience a break from watching the rest of the cast, all children.

Performed at the recital, the dance began the same way as it did in the prison, but this time they danced in the same space. What had once been a prison cell pantomimed with hands now was a small intimate space they shared together. The tempo changes to all waltz mid song, they danced face to face, but still without hands touching. At an emotional crescendo in the music they touch, and the heat of it sends them flying in different directions where both dance intensely and fast. Finally, they are unable to stay away from each other, and Bethany jumps into Andre's arms.

The dance ends with a fadeout while the two of them are embracing privately, reminiscent of the way teenagers danced in the fifties, just rocking back and forth, arms around each other. A stunned silence followed by a booming standing ovation ended their performance.

After the concert, I got a call from a parent. She was driving the girls in FIF 4—then aged 11, 12, 13 and 14—home. "The kids wanted me to call you and ask you if Andre and Bethany are going somewhere to make mad passionate love?"

"Tell them that's a very rude question! She is his teacher, it's a dance, it's acting! They should know that by now!"

Andre had received parole permission to sleep over since the concert ended after his curfew. When I woke the next morning, Bethany and Andre were still sitting in the living room talking. I took one look at them and I knew they were in love.

"I just want you to know that nothing happened between us. I would not disrespect your house," he said.

Little did he know my old hippie opinion: making love should come with love whenever possible—it's sexier that way—and any couple in my home meeting that criteria I consider a blessing on the house.

Two years later, after being together from that night forward, enduring separations, overcoming parole restrictions, and working out all the kinks, they married.

Getting married at City Hall in New York City is easy. A marriage license costs $35. Twenty-four hours later, the ceremony is performed, which costs $25. Couples arrive by foot, taxi, and subway. There are no reservations available; you simply walk in and take a number just like you would at a deli counter or the DMV and wait until your turn. Bethany spent the night with her sister, and was already in Manhattan. Andre arrived by subway.

I'd only slept four hours the night before, so I was disappointed to be tired on such an important occasion. By noon dozens of hopeful couples were waiting to enter the small chapel and complete the ten-minute ceremony. The large hall was buzzing with dozens of couples about to take the grand leap of faith that is marriage. Cameras and flowers were everywhere. Many women wore white wedding gowns, the hems grimy from the New York City streets. Some couples were in jeans, others in business attire, possibly marrying during their lunch break. One at a time couples were brought into one of two chapels. The wait varied depending on how many couples crowded into the building. Our wait was about two hours.

A dozen or more members of Bethany's large family and a few former prisoners were in attendance. Only the former inmates and Andre's sister represented his side of the family. His mother refused to come because he invited her via text message which she considered impolite. His father, a working man, was ashamed to meet his son's new family dressed in a uniform.

I was there for Bethany, but since Andre had fewer witnesses I counted myself family on his side. He must have caught that vibe, because he clutched me tightly, put his head on my shoulder and wept. I knew at that moment the person he wished to be holding was the beloved grandmother he'd never seen again after leaving Guyana. In that moment I was a surrogate and I was honored. I witnessed the wedding with one half of my shirt soaked with his tears. After the wedding I walked the forty-five blocks from City Hall to Port Authority to catch the bus upstate. I was no longer tired. I'd helped to choreograph a marriage! How many choreographers can say that?

LIFE GOING FORWARD

Bethany was no longer reticent about speaking up, in the prison or anywhere else. Her confidence had taken a quantum leap. When we team-taught at the prison, I sensed my constant interruptions annoyed her, although she did her best to hide it. For years, I'd told her some wonderful opportunity would eventually come her way, and now it did: she was offered a job teaching dance in a high school, at considerable pay.

I was too proud and happy for her to be upset, but not sure what I'd do without her. I could no longer manage, at sixty-five, to demonstrate movements fully. The desire to dance hadn't gone anywhere; the engine was revved and vibrant, but the frame and body lagged behind. Bethany could teach a class as well as I; the only things I felt truly needed for were choreography and philosophy.

I felt marginalized. But I found a cautionary and inspirational tale in the story of Martha Graham, an infamous narcissist who'd reportedly said, "You need to know this is the worst moment of my life" to a young dancer just before she went on stage. The young dancer was performing a solo that was Martha's signature piece in her heyday.

"When I stopped dancing I lost my will to live," Martha wrote in her memoir. "I stayed home alone, ate very little, drank too much and brooded. My face was ruined, and people said I looked odd. Finally, my system gave in. I was in the hospital for a long time, much of it in a coma."

In 1972 she quit drinking, returned to her studio, reorganized her company and went on to choreograph ten new ballets and many revivals. In 1981, at the age of 87, she choreographed *Acts of Light*. Her early works were often built on conflict and emotion. *Acts of Light* is pure beauty, dancers in simple golden unitards moving through the smooth, codified work of a choreographic genius. *Acts of Light* was one of the dances I studied over and over on YouTube.

No longer able to dance, I'd been afraid to choreograph for FIF4, but I was to discover a new and improved direction. Throughout my career, my students had been hampered by my limitations. I'd never developed professional technique, so steps too difficult for me had not appeared in my choreography. Now, I spent hours looking at ballets and writing down movements that appealed, making a half-assed attempt in the privacy of my home studio to mimic the steps. Then I explained the movements through words and gestures while doing whatever I could to still show the movement.

Molly Rust took Bethany's place as my assistant, directing rehearsals and demonstrating choreography. All three Rust sisters, Emily, Molly, and Sophie, danced in successive FIF companies until they graduated from high school. Their mother, Natalie, was a huge fan; she often came to rehearsals and watched from the sidelines. Natalie was a nurse in a woman's health clinic who took excellent care of herself and her family, serving only organic food. She wasn't a stage mother, just a fierce negotiator on her children's behalf, a momma tiger watching out for her kids and making sure they got what they deserved.

When Natalie received a breast cancer diagnosis at forty-two, she asked me to keep her girls dancing until they graduated high school and their company was disbanded. Towards the end, when she was confined to a wheelchair, FiguresInFlight 3 was invited to dance at the National Museum of Dance in Saratoga Springs. Against her husband's and her sister's wishes, she insisted on making the two-hour trip. Her sister begged me to intervene. "She's got a death wish! If she comes to the performance she might die that day!" I did not stop her, nobody could. She died a few months later, at forty-four. Her three daughters were each in different companies, FiguresInFlight 2, 3, and 4, respectively. They stayed until the end.

The dancers in FIF4 were all grown up. It was their last year. Many would be off to college, and I would retire from teaching. Their technique had surpassed that of the previous companies. The majority had what is referred to as "the physical talent," bodies made for dance. And what I criticized in the past, I loved about them now. Their smooth surfaces concealed hearts and souls no less determined and caring than any of the former students. This group would come to experience the most extraordinary dance event in my career.

Chapter 12

Figures in Chains

"How can you work with people like that after what they've done? What about the victims?" Every prison volunteer has faced those questions. It's politically correct in some circles to advocate for nothing but bread and water, and in others to claim to be a bottomless well of superhuman compassion and forgiveness.

The reality is more complicated. Pursuing my dream of teaching in prison at last, bent on Tikkum Olam, I was unconcerned about the victims of the dancers' crimes until—against prison rules, but in line with my personal ones—I'd offered to help one man find pro bono legal help after he'd been denied parole for a second time. He told me he murdered his girlfriend, the mother of his infant child. The reality that these men, men I loved like sons, had done awful things to real people awakened some feeling that had been dormant in me. All that week I struggled with my new knowledge of his deed and with how clueless and unconcerned I'd been about victims. Then it was Sunday again, and I was back inside.

"I didn't know if you would ever talk to me again, after what I told you," he said.

"I didn't either," I told him. This man had become someone admirable. I stayed in the present and was able to move forward. Ever after that, the victims were real to me. Another piece of the puzzle emerged, deepening my comprehension; it became easier to under-stand the divide between my prison students and the outer world. The fact that they had victims is the only thing that many people know, or care to know, about these men. Keeping them defined by that narrow reality, the worst moment of their lives and the lowest that is in them, never brought a single victim back to life, dried a family member's tears, or rehabilitated a damaged soul. To do better, people must know better.

We seldom hear about it in the free world, but a lot of prisons have charity groups. At Woodbourne, it's common for inmate organizations to donate to myriad causes: local food pantries, gifts for inmates' mothers on Mother's Day, Christmas presents for the children of inmates who can't afford to buy any, aid to victims of natural disasters. Often these donations come out of the men's scarce commissary money, representing a sacrifice of the few small creature comforts available.

I believe it was at Greenhaven where a prisoner read an article about a girl who needed an operation. He took it upon himself to go and solicit funds from many prisoner-run organizations. We raised a few hundred dollars and gave the money to her family.

When I was at Collins, upstate, a group of us with an officer did community service outside of the prison. We went to churches, hospitals, day care centers, did whatever was needed. One time we worked outside for thirty days, a whole month, Monday through Friday. That felt like a real job. We went to Niagara Falls, we repaired structures in the park and cleaned the walkways.

During a lunch break I watched the children playing. It was so good just to be like a regular person, enjoying the beauty and innocence of the children. It was so helpful to be with ordinary people, work on my ability to interact with others since all my interactions were with other prisoners and staff. We weren't shackled, people were kind to us. It gave me a sense of pride, I still belonged in the world, and I could be useful.

There are vital lessons that no book can teach, that cannot be told with words. To learn to love the light, you need to know what it feels like to walk in the dark.

Mention prison charity and some correction officers scoff. "They're just trying to look good for the parole board." Imagine for a moment that your every well-intended deed was met with that reaction. How many of us would continue to try? When I mention teaching dance to prisoners, I get disbelief. Even people who realize that there needs to be more to incarceration than bread and water and breaking rocks often find it strange that a real criminal would dance in prison. Shouldn't those people stay focused on basic literacy? On learning a trade? What will they gain from dancing?

Putting together a prison recital takes two years of intense practice several times a week. Between visits, prison jobs, and other ups and downs, it's impossible to get every student in class every single Sunday. Even though they tell me it helps a bad mood, some men will skip when they're depressed or angry.

Officers, even some of the inmates, will tell me that so-and-so is a totally different person around me than he is the rest of the time; that I am being fooled. Even if this is true, he gets to practice being his best self some of the time.

Families aren't allowed to attend prison dance recitals. Rehab-ili-tation Through the Arts records the performances to DVDs for them, along with interviews with each man to be sent to the families. The dancers are often asked during the interview, what do you get from dancing?

This program has affected me in a major way. Not only has it changed my life, but it saved my life. When it started you would have never heard me say that; once I understood the principles of it, it had power. The principle of the dance program is about attention. Dance is just a platform to teach attention, attention is a synonym for love, when you pay something attention, you are paying love to it.

When I started to pay love to myself, my life became different, I realize you have to pay attention all the time. Even though it's hard; one second that you are not paying attention to yourself and what you are doing can cost you the rest of your life. (Tyrone)

The message I want to give is one of hope, one of believing in dreams and that the world could be better. That you could be better. We have a choice in the way we proceed in life. Depending on that choice, it will either lead you to on a path to sorrow or a path to joy. And I hope just my little part in this performance radiates that choice that I have made. (John)

Within the group, natural leaders emerge. Like Ozzy. Technically he was the only White man in the dance group, but the running joke was that he was superhuman. "Ozzy isn't White, man! He's not part of any race at all. He's from another planet, one where the men have special powers." Ozzy is brilliant at math, science, theater, singing, playing music, and dancing. Although he openly identifies himself as bisexual, and often came to dance class in pigtails, the other men liked him.

He could memorize long sequences of exercises and combinations after seeing them only once, and knew exactly where a particular sequence began in the music. "Starts at 3 minutes and 23 seconds," he'd shout from across the room, amazing since he wasn't close enough to see the exact time on the CD player. He danced without fear, flinging himself around with a vengeance, scaring us all that he'd burst himself into a serious injury. Bethany and I grew to depend on his talents. Then one Sunday Ozzy was gone, transferred to another prison. He left us a note.

Dear Bethany and Susan,

For the past 16 months I have looked forward to no other time of the week as I looked forward to dancing. I am leaving for Clinton Annex near the Canadian border; more than the loss of schooling, more than the loss of friends, more than the distance from my family, I am devastated by the loss of dance class. Each of the other things above can be restarted, replaced, or overcome but unless I walk into a miracle I will have to live without dance class for another 19 months. It sucks because of all the above things, only contact with my wife has allowed me to do the work on myself that dance has.

There is a quality of stillness that precedes all motion—but it is motion, change—that is the demarcation of life. That quality of stillness allows for us to understand the need for motion in a way that creates an appreciation for change. As amazing as presence is, as insightful as such a state of being allows us to be, know that I cannot remain still forever. Stagnation due to the appreciation of stillness would be the truest warlocking—the worst possible outcome or oath-breaking that can occur. Whether I want it or not it is time to flow into the next shape.

If I can pull it off, I will do my best to continue with so much of the training as I know to prepare me for dancing with FiguresInFlight Released. I thank you from the bottom of my heart for being unselfish enough to give dance to myself and the guys, and may bright blessings flow from the Lord and Lady on your lives.

Someday I will be free,

Ozzy

"Someday We'll All Be Free," by Donny Hathaway, was the music for the dance Ozzy had been teaching to several beginners when they came and took him back to his cell, where he was told without warning to pack up his few belongings and get on the bus for the seven-hour ride upstate to the Clinton Annex. We missed him, but such is prison life. A program that he needed to achieve his freedom was offered at Clinton.

Someday ninety-seven percent of all the folks in prison will be free. For them, the wait feels like forever. Armchair observers who cluck at what they consider a short sentence for some crime or other have never themselves experienced a week, a day, a moment, much less years, of confinement. We made dances that spoke to the inmates' pain. Bethany and I choreographed a set warm up to Ryuichi Sakamoto's "El Mar Mediterrani," a work we interpret began in sadness and frustration, then moves through prayer and salvation as the music becomes stronger, and morphs into defiant hope, resolving into soft heart-breaking melodies depicting peace and love. It's the journey we all need to make; one that I wanted them to feel deep within their own substance.

What can prisoners gain from dance? The finest Ivy League education in the world will not prevent selfish behavior or crime, although it may provide the social camouflage to keep one out of prison. Empathy, the antidote to selfishness, springs from somewhere else; it can be seen in the natural empathy of children. Those who aren't lucky enough to get that are faced with walls they must tear down to rebuild healthier personalities, from the ground up and from the gut out. And nothing engages the gut like music and movement.

They speak of a sense of connection to what was was long lost. Some enter prison at sixteen. Jeffery seemed even younger. I do not know about his crime but it had to be serious because of the length of his sentence. The other men intimated in a teasing manner that he was completely inexperienced with women. When he was released he asked several of us volunteers advice about sex. A question that he asked me was surprising, I tried to be polite in my response, "I don't know anything about…." very graphic question. As I write this he is a successful free man for the past 8 years, married with a child. He figured it out, just like Adam and Eve!

"The dance program brought me back to the innocence still within me," said Jeffery. "I am able to be myself in the dance program and have fun. I grew up in a culture where my family danced for everything: birthdays, even when tragedy occurred, to get our minds off of it. In 2000 I lost my mother. We used to always dance together. It's like since then Susan became my mom. I see my mom through Susan, she always encouraged me. Whenever I do any type of dance I always visualize my mom, by the same token, when I dance with my peers I can feel the love radiating through us because we all share a common struggle."

Christian Plant is not his real name. This quote, like all the others, comes from videos; The Game Changer, a program post-prison when they danced at the famed 42nd Y in Manhattan, and from the radio documentary. It's unfortunate that he and I had a falling out over misogynistic social media posts. I make no excuses for that. Suffice to say if they are locked up at 16, they come out at 16, still in the cultural norms of their pre-incarceration religion and culture when it comes to women.

Here's what he said on the stage of the 92 Street Y shortly after his release:

"Dance restored my sensitivity that I have lost throughout my years in prison," said Christian Plant. "Dancing has allowed me to take off the mask, get rid of the façade, not have to conform to the ideas of masculinity; it's helped me challenge ideas about masculinity. Being a dancer! Who would have ever thought of that; be a dancer, especially while in prison! Susan and Bethany have helped me grow in a way that no books have. The dance program has put me back in touch with what I lost and that's love. I dance to cope with the longing for love. It gives me the opportunity to own space; I do not feel bound by the institution of prison when I dance.

"The dance program has helped me gain back a sense of my humanity. I've been in prison almost twenty years now; I have literally spent half my life locked up. When we do certain things in life we lose a sense of our innocence and humanity. Dance has helped me regain that because when I am in class and performing I am not a convicted felon, a person who committed a crime. I am not that son who disappointed his family and hurt so many people."

This sense of becoming a different person while dancing was something most of them explained. "I always had a hard time articulating myself through words," said John. "Dance gave me a way to express myself through movement, through my physical body. For me, that was very valuable. In the street, I would have never thought about dancing. I was always kind of a laid-back sort of guy, smooth, but the dance program gave me the opportunity to transform myself, evolve my personality. It gave me a different way to look at my body, how to look at myself inside of space, an awareness of who I am and how I fit in to the environment."

I had a special bond with John. He was the most intellectually curious and articulate student of them all. He earned an associates degree inside Woodbourne. I was looking forward to continuing the velocity of interesting conversations on the outside. He was honest with me when he told me that he "would not continue talking to me as a free man." At first I was disappointed, but since some men just stopped communicating with no explanation at all, I appreciate John's directness. I wish him well and hope he still moves to music wherever he is now.

Fitting in, in a prison environment, usually entails keeping one's guard up at all times. In prison, kindness is frequently seen as weakness. The very idea of dancing in prison seems crazy to some; no matter what recruiting techniques I try, I never have more than between ten to twenty students, out of a population of hundreds.

I asked the guys how they overcame gender stereotypes, how they found the courage to set aside the macho personas that so many of their peers depended upon for survival. Some didn't see it as a problem. "For me, I'm just a ham sandwich. Nothing was going to deter me," said David James. "As long as I don't have to wear a female wig, we're all right."

The United States puts more people behind bars than any other country, five times as many people compared with Britain or Spain.

It wasn't always like this. Half a century ago, few people were locked up, and those inmates generally served short sentences. But 40 years ago, New York passed strict sentencing guidelines known as the Rockefeller drug laws which put even low-level non-violent criminals behind bars for decades.

David James was a victim of the Rockefeller laws. He had been a very successful drug dealer in what he referred to as the "underground economy." He had rules: certain drugs he would not sell, certain people he would not sell to.

My favorite moment with David James happened in the prison library. The room where I taught dance was not available. Only once was the class conducted in the library. David had something to tell me; A secret. He motioned for me to meet him behind an eye-high stack of books. I leaned into him as close as I could hoping not to be seen. He whispered so low that I could not hear him. Then he raised the volume an inaudible decimal. "I still can't hear you," I whispered. We both burst out laughing.

"Once I got past the peer pressure... I always wanted to do it but there was this stigma, yeah, men don't dance. And then it came to Woodbourne, I'm gonna go ahead and give it a shot, it was different.

Going through the exercises was good for me. Man, these cats don't know what they're missing! This is great!" said Cornell.

Cornel was serving 30 years. My most cherished memory of him was his improvisational dance to the R@B classic Stairway to Heaven.

"Here we go
climbing the stairway to heaven
here we go
walking the road of ecstasy
Taking the load
of this whole world off our shoulders
the door is wide open for you
the door is open for me"

He loved this song. I brought it into every class. He would often deliver a monologue with great humor and poignancy about his impending wedding to someone "unknown but on the way."

"It's really hard to be in prison where you have to be a tough guy all the time, getting up and dancing in front of the whole population," admitted CJ. "At first I said 'I am never going to do this, maybe guys will laugh at me and talk about me.' But Susan taught me it's not going to be like that, the way she taught I don't have that feeling anymore. I don't think like that anymore. I feel free, not bothered. This is positive. The dance program taught me to be myself. I love it." "The way they teach, you're comfortable all the time. You're not afraid to try, or fail. Many of us did not have those safety nets growing up,"

Dancing helps them rebuild a connection between their once-innocent inner selves, their current reality, and their hopes for a better future.

144

CJ was also in college while at Woodbourne. He kept in touch with me and even rode his motorcycle from NYC to New Paltz to attend a Figures in Flight youth company concert. When at the end of the show it was my turn to take a bow, CJ scooped me up and lifted me onto the stage. He has reentered society and has been free 10 years by now.

"Someday I want to show these dances to my grandkids," said Ali. "If they say they can't do it, I'll say 'Look at Grandpa.' Susan says most people learn this when they are little. I'm thirty-four, and look at me! It's hard to stay sane in here, but that's what dance does. We practice being sane. We dance in front of a brick wall, we don't got no mirrors, we don't have nothing to see how we move. We go by what Susan and Bethany tell us. 'You ain't doing this right, bend down, point your toes.' You get the sense that this means something, it's not just that we are criminals. When we perform we are somebody. We are human."

Ali was also a college student inside. By the time a prisoner gets into a prestigious sought-after college program and is willing to perform modern dance in front of other prisoners, he is already rehabilitated. The slogan for Rehabilitation Through the Arts is, "RTA saves lives" I find this offensive. Prison programs provide tools, if they use what is provided they save themselves. When the men credited me with saving them I often used this analogy, if I give you really useful tools to build a house and you build it, was it me who built the house or you?

Many people project upon prisoners the darkest of everything: ne'er-do-wells, society's leeches, inhuman animals. This is so often the way they are portrayed in the media. People will cite poorly understood statistics, retell awful anecdotes, convinced that they've made and prove their case: these men don't and can't change. Certainly, some don't. Simply being punished never made anyone better.

The difference, the missing piece, the other truth, is in what the men describe: emotional literacy; which means paying attention, which is the verb in loving. The men I know are trying to redeem themselves by doing as much good in prison as possible. Given the tools, given an internal way to feel differently about themselves, they can grow up in ways prison rarely provides.

Not every student stays with the program. Some are merely curious. One of my recruitment tactics is my annual presentation at the Black History Month program. I present a history of Black dance in America, complete with video clips; the men perform, and I deliver a rousing speech about the benefits of dance.

Sometimes I get someone like Biz. The night I met him, he was sitting directly in front of the podium during my Black history speech. I lifted up a styrofoam cup full of water and the bottom fell out.

"Your water broke," Biz said.

"Well, that would be a miracle," I replied. Everybody laughed.

I was a little surprised when Biz showed up at dance class. He was older, not in good shape, and complained of aches and pains while dancing, but the men really liked him and so did I. I'd been cautioned to demand perfect manners and gratitude, but Biz amused me by being impolite and hilarious. He was refreshing, but I knew he respected me. "Prison is a jungle," he said. "Knifings, fights and more things going on ....Of course this class is not a jungle, it's a dance class, it's a forest, just a nice place inside of a jungle." Woodbourne was pretty civilized; its nickname within the system is "Goodbourne" for the relative peace and comfort, but Biz had come from other prisons. He didn't last too long, quit dancing, and was transferred to another facility. I was sorry to see him go.

I was often asked to write letters to the parole board when a dancer was approaching his first chance at freedom. The system of parole is antiquated and torturous for the men, waiting twenty or thirty years for five minutes in front of the board where they must convince three strangers of their remorse, transformation, and worthiness. A parole board member I once chanced to meet in the lobby on her way to a hearing said, "We hardly look at the parole letters and paperwork. We decide when the guy walks in and sits down whether we will let him out or not."

"What do you judge that on?" I asked.

"A vibration," she said.

The men say the parole commission only lets out those they know will reoffend and return.

"It's all about job security, keeping up the numbers." The least likely recidivists are men who started their bids between the ages of sixteen and twenty-four, were charged with a violent crime, and have served more than twenty years; this describes most of the men in the dance program. I didn't believe this category of men were the least likely to be paroled until it was confirmed by a retired parole commissioner. He added that sometimes a phone call would come from the "higher-ups," stating that beds needed to be filled and not to let anyone out. One man told me that during his parole hearing he'd anticipated for decades and prepared for months in advance, the parole commissioners were eating their lunch.

Usually about twenty men come up for parole at each hearing. They are all seen in one day; most are denied, and about four are granted. Occasionally this is reversed, sixteen men making it and four denied; this usually happens when the board members, political appointees with sizeable salaries, are retiring and have nothing to lose by showing mercy and compassion. Like so much everywhere—public schools, arts organizations, charities—everything depends on the quality of each individual's consciousness. Some of the board members do care, take time, and believe in second chances. Others don't want to risk their reputation and position. It's easier to keep a man locked up than make a wrong decision with blow-back consequences on the board.

The men spend months preparing their parole packets. David's folder was so carefully constructed it was a work of art. It included a carefully worded letter from me. There are rules regarding parole letters. I knew that if I directly said, "I recommend him to be paroled, please parole, it is my opinion he should be paroled," or anything close, my letter would wind up in the garbage pail.

I am writing this letter of reference on behalf of inmate David "Perez" who is being reviewed for parole.

For the last 2.5 years I have known Mr. Perez in my capacity as a volunteer from RTA (Rehabilitation Through the Arts). In addition to volunteering in three area prisons during the previous eight years I am the director of FiguresInFlight dance company, a professional company and school. I am a lecturer on issues pertaining to learning and I travel throughout New York State conducting artist in residency programs in the public schools. I have worked with 10,000 children and adults in my long career and I trust my ability to judge character. I also lecture and teach a philosophy of self-evolution, self-scrutiny aimed at producing positive change based on the practice of paying and training attention.

Mr. Perez volunteered for the dance program and has performed three times with an audience from the general population. Modern dance in a men's prison is certainly unusual and all the inmates have received some criticism from others for participating.

I have taught the therapeutic dance and philosophy class to Mr. Perez for over 300 hours, during the last 2.5 years, on every Sunday, all year long. Mr. Perez has overcome a lot of adversity to join the program. He is 44 years old and has spent most of his life incarcerated. Modern dance was a new, unfamiliar experience for him. He struggled with learning choreography and doing exercises more fitting for a much younger person. He was helpful to the other men, showed leadership ability, his attendance was consistent. Good attendance shows self-discipline, a much needed quality should the board decide to release him.

When Mr. Perez first went to prison, so many years ago, he could not read or write. He took it upon himself to become educated and I am often amazed at the degree of intellectual information he has mastered. If I mention a book, concept, artwork, he is often familiar with it.

Mr. Perez has availed himself of every program that time would allow him to attend. He holds many certifications, completed his GED, and has attended vocational classes in addition to a massive amount of independent study.

Mr. Perez is educationally driven and passionate about self-development. Since I have known him he has made many profound changes, working to become a better person.

It is my opinion that Mr. Perez has the capacity to lead a useful productive life.

Sincerely yours,
Susan Slotnick

Only once was my letter cited in a parole hearing. They told him he was granted his freedom because of my letter.

In regards to inmate Omar Robertson #99A2380
Attention: Deputy Franco
99 Prison Rd.
Woodbourne, NY 12788

I am writing this letter of reference on behalf of inmate Omar Robertson who is being reviewed for parole.

For the last 2 years I have known Mr. Robertson in my capacity as a volunteer from RTA (Rehabilitation Through the Arts). In addition to volunteering in three area prisons, I also lecture and teach a philosophy of self-evolution, self-scrutiny aimed at producing positive change based on the practice of paying and training attention.

I have taught Mr. Robertson dance and philosophy for a total of 500 hours over the past two years since I volunteer in the prison for approximately five hours a week, every Friday and Sunday, all year long. Not one man who has participated in this program and has been released has returned to prison. This is not because of the program. Men who volunteer for a modern dance program in prison are already way down the road to rehabilitation. They are made fun of by many in the general population which requires a strong sense of self. Omar is an individual, confident and sure of himself. He did not start out that way.

Of all the men I have instructed, Omar has traversed the greatest distance from who he was two years ago to the man he is today. He was painfully shy. It was impossible for him to speak in public since when he was a boy. His speech was delayed. At the last performance he recited a prepared speech in front of 300 men from the general population.

But dance is not his main interest in the RTA dance program. It is the philosophy that captures and holds his attention. He enthusiastically grabs on to all ideas that will help him become a better person. He works hard, rarely missing a class. This quality of "being your word" and following through with attention and discipline is certainly needed to re-enter society and be a productive citizen.

Over time I have written many letters and also refused to write many. If the board in their wisdom decides in his favor, I believe he has the chance for a second life filled with service to society.

Thank you for your consideration of Mr. Stiles. Please add this letter to his file.

Sincerely,

Susan Slotnick

In the case of David Perez my letter did not help; he was denied. David stopped coming to the dance class. When a man gets hit with two more years before his next parole hearing, he faces the same place, same people, same rules, still locked up, and the devastation of circumstances that cannot change; brutal sameness made all the more bitter by failed hope. All he can do is switch programming; ask for a different work assignment or a transfer to another facility. David requested a transfer to a prison where it was rumored parole was easier to achieve.

When David was fifteen, he'd fallen in love with a neighborhood girl named Tina. He went to prison at eighteen; in the throes of first love, Tina vowed to wait. David refused; he wanted her to have a better life. She was too young to make such a promise.

Tina left for college, and David married twice in prison; the second time he married someone he met in the prison visiting room. Tina also married. Yet they always wrote. At one point, they didn't see each other for six years, but the relationship deepened, and she began to visit him often. They realized they had never stopped loving each other and believed they would, in the end, marry and be together for the rest of their lives.

When I first contacted Tina she was in the midst of ending a relationship and hoping that David, who was approaching the end of his twenty-six-year sentence, would soon be free.

David's transfer request was denied. Once in a while David would come to dance class to see the new choreography, although he no longer participated. His absence was a loss, since his dancing was nothing short of magnificent.

Fifteen years of prison Sundays, and I know what to expect. I arrive home in the early evening and by nightfall the demons come: chronic weltschmerz, anxiety about the fate of a particular prisoner, fears—mostly imaginary—for my daughters, my husband, myself, the world. And because of my state, I am attracting more negative energy. Bad news often comes on Sunday night: a phone call, email, or Facebook message that ratchets up the chaos. This email arrived from Tina on a Sunday evening.

Hello Susan,

I hope you have been doing well. I'm writing to inform you that David has been very sick & in the hospital for the past 3 weeks. He hadn't been feeling well for a few months. He's so hard headed that he wouldn't go to sick call. When he finally did go, they did blood work. I saw him on May 30th & he was jaundiced. I insisted that he go back to medical. When he did go the following day he was rushed to the emergency at Albany Medical Center. They began doing a ton of tests. They put a stent in from his liver to alleviate backed-up bile. While the surgeon was inserting the stent he ran into something that was blocking him from moving forward. Under further investigation they discovered that it was a tumor. All the tests came back that the tumor was cancerous. David has cancer. The doctors wanted to remove it and administer chemotherapy. Before they did, a laparoscopic exploration and a biopsy were done. A few days later he was told that they can no longer operate, the cancer is already spread & he is now classified as terminal.

This has been a devastating blow for him, for all of us. He is all alone. He can only make 1 phone call a week. That broke my heart. This hospital is so strict. They wouldn't allow me to even see him. I drove up

4 hours and they only allowed his brother, sister & aunt in. I had to call a lot of people at the facility to finally be granted visitation. I saw him this past Friday. He was so happy to see me. He is determined to fight; he is a fighter.

His aunt is his emergency contact, we are not married. The hospital will not allow anyone, not even his aunt an opportunity to talk to his doctors. He has rights that are being denied! My heart is heavy. I feel helpless. No matter what I get shut out by the hospital.

I'm going to get information about a medical release. Maybe he can apply for that. It should be granted since they say he is terminal.

My faith is strong. I believe that everything happens for a reason. I believe that God is going to heal him as long as David feels he deserves to be healed. I tell him he's got to turn this test into his greatest testimony.

Susan, if there is any advice you can give that can help him please don't hesitate to let me know. Please keep him in your prayers.

Thank you,

Tina

Several emails passed between us, mostly regarding the astronomical cost of lawyers if he was turned down for medical parole and needed to mount an appeal. The initial retainer would be ten thousand dollars, with more fees accumulating after that.

Months earlier, the department of corrections granted permission for a radio documentary to be made during dance class. A photographer had accompanied the interviewer. She was cautioned to take still pictures only, but her camera had video capability. I convinced her against her will, to film the men dancing an adaptation of Alvin Ailey's masterpiece Revelations: the first movement, the "I've Been 'Buked" section.

Ailey's piece had great meaning for FiguresInFlight inside the walls. Alvin Ailey choreographed this dance in 1960 during the height of the civil rights movement. He wanted to show the dignity and beauty of African American people. The lyrics, "I've been [re]buked, I been scorned," were originally sung by Black slaves. If Alvin Ailey knew prisoners, mostly men of color, victims of mass incarceration were dancing in the style he created, learning the technique he used to teach dancers, he would want these modern-day slaves, Black men in prison, folks misunderstood, scorned and marginalized by society, to carry on the message of beauty and dignity I saw in all of them every time they danced.

"I've Been 'Buked" was David's favorite. It begins in a clump shaped like the letter V; David, always in the apex, danced it without a molecule of pretension, authentic and pure, his movements smooth and clear. Visually, to see a middle-aged man with long dreads moving like a feline creature, expressing the emotions of a person enduring the hardship of prison was astounding. It is for sure a moment that has never happened in a dance performance before. David was not granted medical parole.

I broke the rules yet again and sent the video, its very existence a violation of the rules, to a lawyer with a short note explaining David's predicament. No response.

Another Sunday night, and I received this note from Tina:

Susan,

As of right now we are not going to need to raise any money. 2 lawyers that came from your email sent him a letter. He received it yesterday & they went to see him today! They told him that they are going to do everything within their power to help get him released & their services are going to be provided PRO BONO. This is an absolute GOD SEND. They said it was because of the video of him dancing. That's why they took his case.

It had become a tradition for many of the men on the morning of their release in the dance program to come directly to my house for breakfast before being thrust into a world as foreign to them as it was to Rip Van Winkle on awakening from his twenty-year sleep. Just like Rip, the prisoners discover shocking changes; they often talk about isolation, no one smiling or saying "Hello," everyone consumed by a device. Many have a parent who has died. Faces of family members they pictured over and over while locked up are hardly recognizable. I used to wonder why they wanted to take their first walk of freedom up my driveway when they had families and sometimes children. "They want to be reborn into the world from the mother figure who knows who they are now," offered my daughter Rebekah, "a familiar face from the present, not the past."

David and I often talked about the morning he would get released. We had everything planned, including the menu. Tina would pick him up at 9 a.m. on a Tuesday; we would spend several hours feasting and rejoicing. Then they would leave to renew their life together. Within twenty-four hours David would be required to report to his parole officer and the harsh realities of returning to the community from prison would begin.

A pattern emerged. At first, they call me every day, while sitting around in offices that are supposed to provide services on the outside: meal tickets, housing, funds to get started. One man sat waiting in an office from 9 AM to 7 PM and at the end of the day was told the person he was supposed to see left at lunchtime. The outside world is a complex and demoralizing transition fraught with temptations and obstacles: drinking, drugging, lack of adequate education and job skills, limited housing options, health issues.

Both the men and their families want to recapture the lost years. The families want the son, brother, husband, or father they lost to come home the same person they remember. They are faced with a grown man, a deeply wounded stranger. The men want to make up for lost time, especially with women. Two of the men from the dance program entered prison virgins and came out in a hurry to fix that condition; some got involved too fast, with too many women. I knew of one man in the theater program who went back to prison on a domestic abuse charge.

Men mature physically, intellectually and even spiritually locked up, but prison doesn't provide opportunities for emotional maturity. They can react rather than respond, fall back into habitual teen-aged behaviors fueled by fear and alienation. Prison teaches a scarcity mentality, encourages living in the past or the future. There's no opportunity to learn to be responsible for the emotional life of another in the present, the main requirement of a parent, father or husband. It's hard to learn to be proactive, have a sense of purpose and clear-cut attainable goals, when you're constantly subjected to a threatening environment. As much as they try to seek growth, unity and goodwill with others, opportunities are scarce, self-protection is a constant need.

They do develop skills on the inside that men on the outside often lack. Their ability to observe other people and cut though lies rivals that of Judge Judy. There's a term they use for this, it's called "prison vision."

The time I choreographed a Caribbean dance for Hispanic Recognition Month, the men wanted me to perform it with them.

"I can't. I will make a lot of mistakes, it will take attention away from you, and the audience is full of men I don't know. Shaking my seventy-year-old self in front of them will make me self-conscious."

"Bullshit," said Rahkeem. "The first two things are true, the third is a lie."

"Yeah man, so true!" "Ha ha, she tried to put one over on us!" General hilarity.

"How'd you know that?" I asked.

"Come on, give us more credit than that! We've been watching you, girl. We know all your tricks, you're never self-conscious about anything, that's just our prison vision, we can see through anyone."

The details these men notice that most men don't! I don't wear make-up. Three times in my life I have purchased the whole shebang, only to put it on once or twice before leaving it in the car. In summer, the heat melted the lipsticks, congealed the face power, dried up the eye liner, and crumbled the rouge.

I tried one more time, determined to use it. No one noticed my eyeliner and lipstick, not my husband, students or friends, until I went inside the prison. When I entered the dance space at Woodbourne you'd have thought I'd had a face lift, tummy tuck, and body transplant.

"What are you wearing make-up for? You don't need that."

"Maybe you look a little fresher, younger, but it's just not who you are. It's fake."

"My grandmother, a full-blooded Navajo Indian, looked like you. Put a serape around her head and she looked great, no need of embellishments."

"You look weird! We don't like it."

David saw through me well. He knew when I was upset or had drunk too much coffee and was hyper, and especially when my mind wandered. "Susan, attention lady, where did you go?" he'd say. He seemed more emotionally mature than many. I believed that with Tina by his side he had a shot at a good life. I asked her to send me some pictures of them together when teenagers. In one picture, they are fifteen, sitting on a couch. She is leaning into him, one arm casually wrapped around his upper thigh, her gesture suggesting physical intimacy. He is smiling, beaming happiness and joy. His face, so young, was unfamiliar. Looking at the photo, I realized that in five years of being with him every week, often twice a week, I had never once seen him smile.

The Department of Corrections granted David a special medical parole hearing. His lawyers were ready to mount an appeal if he was turned down again. Why would they schedule a special hearing and deny him? That made no sense. We all believed it was just a formality.

I should have known better. Nothing in prison makes any sense. Terminal, his time already served, an exemplary record, a support system in place—none of it mattered, there was still no mercy. His hearing was conducted on a screen, no bodies but his in the room, saving money for the department of corrections by reducing travel expenses.

"They never even looked up at me," he told me. "They didn't ask me a single question about my illness. After a few minutes, they cited the nature of my crime as the reason for denial."

After that, David disappeared. His friends inside did not know if he was in the hospital or had been transferred to another prison. I received this email from Tina.

Dear Susan,

I haven't been myself lately. Since his release was denied I have really been all over the place and nowhere at the same time. David is at Fishkill prison doing the best he can. I wanted him to be somewhere that could medically take care of him, but I see now that Woodbourne was the best place for him emotionally. His best friends/ his brothers were there. He had the support from the entire administration. They all knew him & truly cared for him. He had many "freedoms" in Woodbourne & was really in charge of taking care of himself, with some independence. So far in Fishkill he is just a number. The staff is uncooperative & rude. He compares the medical ward to being in the solitary confinement. But it's only been a week; I hope things will get better for him.

The lawyers are working on his appeal & trying to get Fishkill to start filling out a new round of medical release paperwork. Submitting a new medical release request is his only hope. The appeal can take many months. I miss him terribly. This is the longest we have been apart over the past 2 years & we are both feeling it. I will let you know how my visit goes. My faith is still strong. We WILL get through this.

Hope everything is good with you.

Tina

David resurfaced briefly at Woodbourne. He came to class and rather dispassionately told us the medical details of his case, watched rehearsal, and left. We had a performance for the general prison population, about three hundred prisoners and twenty outside guests coming to be in the audience. He hadn't danced in many months. He'd lost thirty pounds. Nevertheless he asked to perform his favorite dance, I've been Buked , the first movement in Alvin Ailey's masterpiece, Revelations. Normally he was pristine in appearance; he even ironed his t-shirts and sweatpants. He was in no condition to perform but I gave him the coveted position in the front at the apex of a triangle.

Disheveled and limping after the dance performance, he was asked to speak by a friend watching the show from the gym bleachers where the prisoners sat:

Many of you guys don't know that in June I was diagnosed with stage four cancer, terminal, they gave me one year. (A man for the general population watching the show says, 'Take your time man, we're all with you, don't worry about it.' David continues.) My family has been my rock, my friends I don't know what I'd do without ya, the staff you guys put me in for medical parole, and they approved me [copious applause] it's not over yet, I go to the board August 11, so fingers crossed they are giving me a shot, I'm hopeful,. But by the same token, 26 years ago, I took a man's life, Mr. Levent. I can't forgive that, so I am hoping and praying that they show me the compassion that I didn't show him, and with that I would like to say thank you.

At least for a few weeks David could hope for a different outcome.

Shortly after he was turned down for medical parole his lawyers secured him another hearing. By the day of the new hearing he was in the hospital. Tina was told the cancer had spread to his pancreas and there was nothing more they could do for him; a different doctor gave her conflicting information, driving her crazy.

The parole board conducted the hearing at his bedside. I was told by Jean King that that "never" happened. He was granted parole and promptly freed. He is a fighter. No doctor is God, one doctor says one thing, another doctor something else. He will dance again.

That was my hope. This is what happened. The phone rang at 9 a.m. on a Tuesday. I heard the sound of traffic in the background. "Hello Susan, this is David."

For an instant, the cancer was forgotten and all that remained was the glee that comes from the first phone call, a ritualistic passage from confinement to freedom, a simple right taken for granted by free people, his first privilege. In my mind's eye I saw Tina and David, windows open, wind flushing out the years of painful separation while David made phone call after phone call to friends and family.

He asked me to visit as soon as possible. When the day and time for the planned reunion came Tina said he was not doing well. He was hospitalized. I should not come.

My annual residency at Newcomb Central Schools took me to the Adirondacks for a week. Liam Appelson, home from Yale for the holidays, was my assistant. The residency was extremely intense. We taught the entire school and mounted a performance, all in three days.

I arrived home on Friday night exhausted. I planned to see David, already in hospice care, the following Monday. My plan to spend all of Saturday recovering in bed was abruptly abandoned when Tina called at 7 a.m. and told me Monday might be too late.

For all my accomplishments and strong surface, I am dependent on Sam in myriad ways. He drove me everywhere, but at 6 that morning he had left for a ski trip to Colorado. I was on my own. The highways on Long Island are notoriously perilous, crack-ups, sirens, traffic jams intermingled with fast cars changing lanes rapidly in heavy traffic. I had not driven to New York City in twenty years, and never to Long Island. I white-knuckled it, heart pounding, scared to change lanes in the heavy traffic, trying to make the switch slowly while drivers slammed on their brakes, honking their horns, disgusted by my lack of initiative and courage.

Tina and I met for the first time in the parking lot. We hugged, cried, both of us drained, stunned, and sad. Just like in India, reality was less frightening to me than what I imagined, David was not scary at all; even in his suffering, he was quite beautiful. As I had experienced at the bedsides of Hugo and my brother Steven, the hours took on a quiet calm. David was in and out of sleep, so the visit was primarily between Tina and I.

If I behaved with my husband's friends like I did that day, I would be considered brazen or crazy. Reunions with released prisoners are celebrated with constant platonic kissing and hugging, exuberant to finally be able to defy the no touching rules. There's nothing sexual in these exchanges of affection. It's about knowing the pain of restricting expressions of love.

I sat on the bed with David. He gestured toward my legs and Tina said, "He wants you to put your legs around him." Which I did. When it was time to say goodbye there was no drama, as if we would all meet again soon although we knew the truth. The ride back was just as harrowing. Even on familiar roads, I managed to get lost three times, winding up at one point on a highway headed back to New York City.

David died on Monday. Tina had a dream in which a tropical bird landed on her head, David cradled her in his arms and told her not to be frightened of the bird. Even though she couldn't see it, the bird was beautiful. I took her dream to mean although we are frightened of death, it might just be beautiful, like the sights in India, the quiet sadness of bedside vigils, the beauty of a calm lake on a grey day.

Several weeks later I began a painting of two figures hugging each other. Tina saw the painting in its beginning stages posted on my Facebook wall. "I don't know whether to tell you this Susan, but those two figures are exactly like a photo of David and I when we were young. Did you see the picture, was that conscious or just in your psyche?" It wasn't conscious then, but it is now. I added a new image to my painting vocabulary, a beautiful bird. I painted Tina and David's faces into the painting and gave it to her.

Chapter 13

⸎

Word is Out

I was eager to share what I learned about prisoners with the public, their articulate speech, their passion to be of service in the larger society and their sensitive dancing. I was invited to Bennington College to show *Reflections of Our Lives Through Dance*, a video of a performance from inside Woodbourne, give a talk and answer questions.

The magnificently maintained 440-acre campus was its own perfect world. My presentation was in the performing arts building. The enormous well-lit pristine clean dance studios were grander than I could have ever imagined: huge, high ceilings, shiny wood or parquet floors, mirrors everywhere. Bennington's state of the art dance facilities are available to students around-the-clock, and include a 10,000-square-foot fully equipped black box theater. Dance classes are accompanied by live music, pianos and drums.

I wondered if the work done in the dance studios came close to matching the grandeur of the space. I thought about our "dance studio" in the prison. A reflection off a glass window that opened onto a dark hallway is our only "mirror," old broken-down chairs make do as barres. Ancient filing cabinets in haphazard heaps line the grimy, dull green walls. Since CDs and DVDs could be broken into usable weapons, any music I brought in had to be transported by an officer; we had a junky old CD player and an ancient VCR. Before every class, the men mopped the floor, using mops from janitorial closets they needed permission to enter. So why, I asked myself did the Bennington students get what they got? Before I met any of the students I had already built up an attitude of resentment. A mere accident of birth had brought them a level of luxury beyond anything the prisoners could haven envisioned in a dance space.

Tuition, room, and board at Bennington costs nearly $60,000 a year.

I presumed the students would all be privileged and blasé. I was wrong. The students were modest, appreciative, interested in and moved by the presentation. Bennington requires that students spend a term at work in the world each year, researching and engaging in acts of social justice. I filmed the student's responses during my talk, and showed it to the men the following Sunday.

"You represented us well," said Tony Singh.

It never crossed my mind that I would become known for making dances in prison. I knew other dance teacher/ choreographers who were willing to network, and self-promote. I like attention and success too, but I wanted it to come without the need to make boring efforts to attain it. To my amazement one serendipitous event after another catapulted the dance program into the public arena. David Gutnick asked to go inside the prison, record a class, and interview the men. To my surprise the Department of Corrections granted permission.

David came to social justice at a young age. The son of two social workers, his dad had grown up in an orphanage, and his mom was the daughter of Icelandic immigrants. We hit it off right away. I asked David how he'd found me.

"I was in New York City doing other stories, and I had free time," he said. "I scanned various events in New York and read about a conference at John Jay College on politics and the arts. There were many professors talking, boring radio material, but also an evening performance of FiguresInFlight Released, former convicts dancing. I saw the performance. It blew me away. I phoned my producer and said I had a story. She said the real story she wanted was the one inside the prison. I looked for you and found you. I am a story teller by nature, a humanist by temperament and belief. I love the arts, painting, dance, poetry and music. They are doors to the human soul.

"I had been in prisons before. My dad was a social worker in a provincial jail in Saskatchewan, my mom was a parole officer. As a journalist, I covered various stories in jail. I knew what to expect once inside. I had one chance to get them to tell me their stories, 15 seconds to prove that I can be trusted. The right body posture, eye movements, and facial expressions will or will not elicit trust. Getting good sound quality, forming instant intimate relationships so what they say into the microphone will be believed by listeners. I think on my feet, get eye contact, and challenge when they go off a truthful message track, saying what they think I wanted to hear."

The Sunday Edition Transcript, August 2013
Documentary on Dance in Prison—*Figures in Flight*
by David Gutnick

For the past seven years dance teacher and choreographer Susan Slotnick has been teaching dance to inmates in a medium security correctional facility in Woodbourne, New York. . . . She says dance saved her from a traumatic childhood. Dance is not a miracle cure for prisoners, just one more way that can help them better understand themselves.

Susan Slotnick lives in a tree-shaded bungalow that shouts 'I believe in art' as soon as you step through the front door. It is the kind of home you would expect to find in the bustling university town of New Paltz, New York. Books and magazines about dance, about drawing, about philosophy and religion fill shelves and tabletops. Susan's own paintings cover the walls: They are colorful, unusual and disturbing. In one a man stares straight out, challenging you to stare back while he bends prison bars with his bare hands. In another, men dance away from their cells, twisting gracefully through space. Susan is sixty-eight years old. She looks a decade younger. She has taught dance to several generations of children; with humor and quick wit she brings good posture, proper foot position, and more than a little discipline into their lives. But it's the guys in the paintings on the walls that Susan credits with giving her life meaning. They are convicted murderers, drug dealers and sex offenders. Some have spent more than half their lives behind bars. They are also Susan Slotnick's prize students.

Thick steel doors are buzzed open. Guards lead a dozen men—in their baggy prison sweats—into a classroom. Chairs and tables are pushed aside. For six hours Susan leads them through exercises and dances until their muscles ache and she is satisfied they have the moves down pat. Then they sit in a circle and talk. Susan calls it her 'philosophy class.' Together they are preparing a performance they will give in front of 800 fellow inmates.

Here is our feature documentary this week: *Figures in Flight*.

Ozzy Mantis said, 'The whole first minute we stand chest raised, every muscle so tight, staring up to the heavens and at the same time staring internally. Even as the lyrics go, "I have been 'buked, I have been scorned," that there is nothing that can make you give up the beauty in oneself. Unless you allow it. We don't allow it. Drop into a full second position plié, extending the right arm outwards, pulling the left in. Reaching to the side, lowering yourself slowly, in the most graceful motion possible, showing that yes, I have been 'buked, you have tried to bring me down, but I am still holding myself up. Left arm out right arm coming in as you go into a deep second position plié. And your hand comes up, reaching for whatever it is that you believe in to help you reinforce yourself if you ever have doubts. And you rise to it. You rise to it and you draw yourself back up to it.'

'Dance shows you that no matter what you do, you have a choice. It teaches me how to interact. My bad choice was that I didn't communicate. I didn't seek out help. So now I learned from that mistake. I learned that I am not here by myself. This world does not exist around Albert. Albert exists in this world.' (Albert Fermin)

'I'm 44 years old. I came in here when I was 18. 25 years for homicide. In the Bible it states that as a child I did childish things, as a man today I do man things. The proof that I have changed is the manner in which I dance.' (David Navarro)

Millions of people heard the broadcast. David Gutnick won three top awards for the program, including the much-coveted Gabriel Award for radio documentaries.

I received emails and comments from all over the world. Strangers called me a saint and a genius. Each time I heard the compliments I thought about my mother-in-law, and the choice I'd made in her life. I knew the truth about myself. Working in the prison was easy, fun, and brought me happiness. If I had allowed Edith to live and die in the home she gave us, maybe I would be praiseworthy for making a sacrifice that was difficult; "I wish I could have a do-over" still pops into my head whenever I think about her. Yet with every acid wave of remorse, I realized how much worse it must be for the men, most of whom had taken a life when a teenager without fully developed brains. No do-overs for them. No do-overs for any of us.

I brought the radio program into the prison for the men to hear. Sitting in a circle, heads bowed, eyes closed, they listened to their own words with reverence. I read them the comments posted on the CBC website, including the few negative ones. They were awestruck that their words reached millions of people.

The radio show was only the beginning. Whether the writers at *Dance Studio Magazine* heard the broadcast or just searched around the internet looking for a subject, I do not know. They wrote a feature published along with pictures of my paintings that were described on the radio show. A year later they gave me the magazine's annual Caring Heart Award. I was honored in the *Huffington Post* during Woman's History Month, featured in both *Dance Magazine* and *Dance Teacher Magazine*.

Now and again I Googled myself just to see how many entries were listed. I know where the fascination with the attention came from: feeling unloved, flunking out of high school. Will I die still not over the hurt from my youth? Can I ever shake it? Does anyone ever? I think not. That little girl, Susan Meltzer, still wants to say to everyone who did not believe in her, "See what I did! You were all wrong about me!" I am talking to ghosts. "You see what I did, you are wrong about me," is what I need to tell myself. I am the only one listening. It's just me who knows the failures of the past, the efforts of the present, and the hope of the future.

I started to receive Facebook messages and emails from strangers who read the articles or heard the radio broadcast:

> I am 72 years old and I remember being a little girl who danced throughout the day. I was a ballerina. I was a tap dancer. I was an interpretive dancer. I grew up. I had a stroke. Can you direct me to information and instruction, either on YouTube or some other similar site, where I could begin to dance again? What are the basic moves I should practice? I do not remember and anyway, then, I made it all up. I heard you on the radio. If I was to look for classes in my area, what would I ask for? Do you have

a video telling us the poses to practice? I would like to dance again. I would like to dance to the end of my life.

＊ ＊ ＊

Hello Susan, I'm a freelance NPR producer, my name is Chris R. The program that is interested in your story is *Destination DIY* out of Oregon Public Radio. The show is focused on individuals taking on creative projects independently, so my interest is in FiguresInFlight and how you facilitated the group's creative direction and growth. I would like to conduct interviews with you and the other members of the dance troupe. Please let me know of your availability.

Mr. R was young, still in his twenties, and although I was not motivated to have another class in the prison disrupted, I promised myself to help young people starting out when possible. Once again, to my surprise, DOC granted him permission to go inside. I asked for one condition: do not ask the men about their crimes.

With David Gutnick I hadn't needed to make this request. His integrity was so obvious it wasn't necessary. The public thirst for salacious crime stories can be satisfied by reality crime shows on television; I wanted the focus to stay on dance.

Mr. R. took each man, one at a time, into another room to interview while I taught the class. Men in prison are so grateful and anxious to please any "civilian" who shows an interest. They don't like to refuse any requests.

I should have known by R's pale, frightened expression that something was wrong. On the drive back to New Paltz Chris R. looked shaken up, off center.

"They seem so nice, but they did such horrible things," he said.

Knowing how unsettling a first visit inside a prison can be, I spent the ride comforting him.

In the final documentary, each dancer announced his crime for the world to hear. I confronted Mr. R. He told me that his producer had insisted that the men tell their crimes on air.

"So, you knew this going in? You purposely ignored my one condition?"

"Yes," he said. "And anyway, their crimes are a matter of public record."

He'd given me his word. I'd trusted him.

On the transcript, the men announce their given names and stated their charges.

Manslaughter in the first, attempted murder, attempted murder in the first, and gun possession.

Statutory rape, rape and inability to consent, commonly known as date rape, possession of an explicit sexual performance involving a child and a misdemeanor count of forcible touching.

One man was a bit more vivid. "I got into a heated debate, and I pulled out my knife and stabbed him."

Not only did the public find out their crime, but I did too. Although it is public record, I never looked any of their crimes up online.

That was the first time in all the years of helping young people, in and out of prisons, that my trust was broken. But I refused to allow the incident to make me suspicious. Whoever Mr. R. is and will become, there's nothing I can do about it beyond the talking to I gave him on the gift of integrity.

I am often asked if I trust the prisoners. I trust everyone until they show me I cannot. Since Mr. R I have helped every young person who contacted me. I will not allow one betrayal to change my philosophy.

Chapter 14

Welcome to the World

"Friend request." It sounds so nice, so *friendly*. Is someone looking for me? That holds an element of mystery and intrigue; the possibility for surprise, an old lover, a high school friend, a stranger offering an opportunity? I studied the photo that came with this friend request; a beautiful young Indian woman in a sparkling sari, dark eyes smiling. She didn't remind me of the women in India in 1969; she was too glamorous, her smile too bold. I decided she must be selling sex. But for some reason I didn't hit the delete button that would have dropped her back into the sea of millions.

The request from a stranger in a sari, who I was sure was selling sex, remained undeleted for days. I always delete friend requests from people with whom I have no friends in common, or send a message asking, "Do we know each other?" At that moment in time, Facebook was charging a dollar to send a message. (There must have been many complaints because several weeks later that was rescinded.) I didn't want to pay a dollar, so I didn't ask her if we knew each other. The beautiful young woman in the sari didn't have a dollar to spare, she simply hoped I would accept her friend request. We almost missed each other over a dollar.

Finally, idle curiosity got the better of me. I clicked on the name. The woman I'd figured for an international temptress turned out to be Indrani Kopal, former video journalist at Malaysiakini, from Kuala Lumpur, Malaysia, a student at the MFA Documentary Program at

Hofstra University. I accepted her friend request and received this message.

> Hi there Ms. Susan, I know a lot about you. I discovered your work last year. The past couple of days, I have been spending time writing a documentary proposal with you as my lead character. I'm a Fulbright grantee, a 34-year-old documentary filmmaker from Malaysia. I am currently enrolled in a two-year grad MFA program in documentary filmmaking. You were my inspiration to write the proposal. I just wanted to thank you for that. I would like to speak with you. I still can't believe you replied to me, I am so thrilled.

A month later I picked Indrani up at the New Paltz Trailways bus station. We hugged, a bit awkwardly. I wish I could write her irresistible lilting accent. We talked for several hours about her documentary proposal. At first, she wanted to find a woman prisoner to profile in addition to me. Unaccustomed to the workings of the American prison system, she thought finding a female in a jail and getting permission to film should be simple.

Even though Indrani arrived in blue jeans and a t-shirt, I assumed that she adhered to the social strictures of her culture. After she disclosed her complicated romantic life, I realized she was sort of a Malaysian hippie, living by her own rules and testing the boundaries. I agreed to allow her to film me in my home and interview my daughters and husband.

She asked me many personal questions, some made me cry. Noticing that I became emotional when talking about my life, she asked, "So, where is all this pain in you coming from?" That was the only question she asked in hours of interviews that made me unsettled. I don't believe I carry more pain than anyone else.

After I told her we'd never get permission to go into women's prison, she decided to rethink her proposal to include the men inside the Woodbourne dance program. But Katherine Vochins refused. RTA had signed a contract with another documentary filmmaker that prohibited the production of a competing film. Indrani had to come up with something entirely new. The paroled dancers had a company of their own now and I had the dancers of FIF4, a cohesive and brilliant troupe, but what could they do together?

Every choreographer has a signature piece, a masterwork. Mine is a twenty-minute drama entitled *Welcome to the World*. The dance was born on a miserable night after a residency day at the Lake Avenue School in Saratoga Springs. Bethany and I had adjoining hotel rooms, and she came in when she heard me weeping.

It was during the first bombing campaign in Afghanistan, and Ahmed the shoe shine boy was on my mind. I met him in 1970 during Sam's and my world tour in Kabul, the city where it looked like everyone had just arrived the day before yesterday. By now we were used to being greeted by the street kids who wait at docks and train stations and airports in poor countries all over the world. That was how I met Ahmed, a nine-year-old Afghani boy with a worn wooden box held together by a rope slung over his shoulder. It was his shoeshine kit; for a small fee, he said, he would shine my shoes.

Sam and I both wore sneakers, so I bought Ahmed a pair of leather shoes at the open market and paid him to shine his own shoes every day. It was a game we played with gesture and laughter.

If he has survived, Ahmed would be 64, surpassing the average life expectancy of Afghani men by twenty years. I've wondered what became of that laughing, industrious child. He would have been 19 in 1979, when the Soviet Union invaded his country. Did he become a Mujahadeen, a freedom fighter? Did he fight for the Taliban? Was he killed later, in an American bombing raid? Did he spend his life in Kabul, or did war, famine, drought, or other adversities push him north, to Mazur-i-sharif, or south, to Kandahar? Did he marry and know the unveiled face of a wife? Did deprivation harden him and make him cruel to her, like the Taliban fighters we read about in the news? Did he ever think of the crazy laughing hippie girl who paid him to shine his own shoes? Would our bombing campaign, just begun, cause his demise?

After a couple of glasses of wine, looking at a picture of Ahmed and me smiling together, I replayed an image of him dying beneath an American bomb. The sad, ironic doublespeak, Operation Enduring Freedom, reminded me of the Vietnam War-era slogans about "making the world safe for democracy." It was all such lies, and so unstoppable.

Bethany sat on my bed and listened to a rant about Ahmed, which grew into a diatribe about the world. As my burst of rage subsided, it turned into consternation about the ever-changing dichotomies that define life on this mysterious planet. "Welcome to the world, this awful crazy wonderful, beautiful, tragic, comedic place," I said. "'Welcome to the World,' that would be a terrific title for a dance!" Memories of my trip around the world came back inspiring the ideas for the dance.

I listened to *Tubular Bells*, the debut album of English musician Michael Oldfield. Oldfield was only nineteen when he made the record, not much older than the dancers in FiguresInFlight, far younger than the prisoners I knew, about the same age as young soldiers I had met in Thailand.

I laid on my back with my eyes closed and let the memories and music create pictures in my mind. Throughout the twenty-six-minute recording, the mystery of creative alchemy took over and a dance appeared before my inner gaze.

WELCOME TO THE WORLD

A group of little children and young adult dancers stand in a clump. When the music begins, all slowly and firmly lift their arms and make a peace sign. But the music is ominous, not hopeful. It signals a warning: We better have peace or else.

A homeless person comes onstage. One at a time, dancers react to her with scorn. A dancer sweeps a human being across the floor. Many different characters, created by the dancers themselves, walk across the stage in a street scene. With each music change, there is a montage of seemingly unrelated events—people genuflect to a guru, as I once did with a teacher before he fell from grace; a group of soldiers, acting like silly Keystone Kops, literally knock themselves out saluting.

The music connotes violence. The war has become deadly. Upstage the movement is repetitive and mechanical, while downstage, two tender duets—one between a soldier on leave with his love, the other between a father and son—are played out against the war's sinister backdrop.

A young girl encounters a magical beast, shaped like a dinosaur but comprised of moving bodies. The beast swallows the child then the beast slowly melts and dies, as a group of ingenuous teenage women, concerned only about their appearances, engage in irritating interplay with the male dancers.

Suddenly everybody is dancing the polka, changing partners as they go, each time leaving one person out. A boy turns into a rock star and is worshiped, screamed over, and rejected in a time-lapse version of manufactured celebrity. All the dancers begin to imitate the rock star, frantically playing air guitar.

The culmination of the dance begins. The dancers begin to transform their movements into a combination that is deeper, more genuine, but incomplete: one hand is still ferociously playing air guitar while the rest of the steps are more vulnerable and authentic. A bell rings, a warning, reprising the mood at the beginning of the dance. The dancers form a line based on the labyrinth exercise we do in class, in which each dancer gazes with neutrality at one person after another until the higher emotional centers of compassion, gratitude, and empathy emerge. At the zenith of the exercise, the recognition that we are all the same, that there are not many separate lives but one same spark of life inside of everyone, transforms the characters into a better version of their ordinary selves. A clump gathers, stage right, while one dancer at a time is lifted up and lowered into the waiting arms of the others to create, as one audience member put, "rebirth for each person and maybe for the world".

My vision, different from that of the audience member, for the end of *Welcome to the World* was to make visible the transforming power that arises in an emergency situation: a natural disaster, the destruction of the World Trade Center, the Boston marathon bombing, the senseless mass killings in Las Vegas. At such times, amidst the horror, an opportunity arises for people to become their best selves, helping and loving one another; so it was in my surreal, episodic dream of a dance. Like all my dances, it shows people at their worst but ends with something good happening. Kind of like *A Christmas Carol*.

The dance was originally choreographed for FIF 2; seven dancers, four boys and three girls. Every time the dance was performed, we got a magical delayed applause: four long seconds of silence followed the final notes, and then thunderous clapping and shouting would erupt. I've read that the first performance of Alvin Ailey's *Revelations* had drawn the same response.

At the time FIF 3 ended, I assumed *Welcome to the World* had been performed for the last time. It surprised me how I accepted this. Since I was unknown, worked with kids, and made no attempt to get my choreography seen by a wider audience, I assumed that my opus was relegated to the dance graveyard along with dozens of others once in the repertory.

But the kids of FIF 4 who had played the young children's parts with FIF 2 and 3 asked to learn it even if it was never performed. They remembered watching the older dancers, and had always found WTTW magical. But with the exception of Liam, they were all girls. WTTW called for a coed cast.

Indrani needed to create two documentaries, a short profile of a person and another, slightly longer, on a subject of her choosing. She asked if there was a project the FIF 4 and FIF Released dancers could work on together.

I don't remember who suggested remounting Welcome to the World with both companies as the solution to both problems at once; it might have been one of the FIF 4 dancers. Beautiful White suburban teens and handsome Hispanic and Black parolees in their thirties and forties dancing together; could I make that work? Did I dare?

I held meetings with the parents. They had reservations and many questions. Had any of the men's crimes involved sex, or been committed against children? Would they be touching each other in the piece? Would they ever be alone together?

The parents trusted me and were supportive of my work in prisons. Since an end-of-the-year recital should include all students, I'd been including the Woodbourne men by using the films made by RTA for years. As the men had been released, they'd joined us live in subsequent concerts and were welcomed by the free FIF community.

"If any one of you has an objection to this project," I told them, "all you need to do is call me. I will drop it immediately, and never disclose who cancelled it." I waited for a call. It never came.

Once it was decided that Welcome to the World would be the "through line" in Indrani's documentary, we began to wrestle with the logistical problems. The men of FIF Released—parolees Andre, Christian, Ali, Luis and others—were committed to the project. Rehearsals had to be in New Paltz, so I had to write each man's parole officer

requesting permission for travel upstate. With food and transportation, each rehearsal would run about three hundred dollars. Including the final performance at McKenna Theatre, that meant at least five
trips, $1500.

Charlie Defria and Alice Andrews, the parents of FIF4 dancers River and Sophie, volunteered to raise the funds. They ran an Indiegogo
campaign, which turned out to be labor-intensive. All of the FIF community sent the link to their contacts and asked them to share, widen-
ing the pool exponentially.

Welcome to the World is a monumental work of modern dance
choreographed by a two-time nominated CNN hero. The dance
promotes world peace and explores the universal human experience through themes of separation, war, suffering, love, and
reconciliation in a compelling 20-minute performance, first
presented on stage to audiences in 2001.

This coming spring, *Welcome to the World* will be rein-
tro-duced with a groundbreaking collaboration of dancers
from two very distinct companies: FiguresInFlight 4 and FiguresInFlight Released.

These two groups of dancers are from sharply contrasting
demographics. One company (FiguresInFlight 4) is made up
of over a dozen teenage high school students from the Hudson
Valley who have danced with Slotnick since early childhood.
The other is comprised of a small group of men who studied
dance while serving time in state prison facilities. Having received intensive dance training under the NYS grant-funded
"Rehabilitation Through the Arts" program, they have since
been released from prison and have continued to dance, forming FiguresInFlight Released, a new company of their own.

The support I was experiencing from my coalition of FIF parents and friends was consistent. I waltzed along, naively believing that the whole world would see the beauty of it. Then an email was sent to the FIF parents, to the *New Paltz Times*, where I am a columnist, to the owner of the building where we rehearse, and to all of our venues:

"Is Pedophilic Content Justified in the Context of Art and Dance?" it was headed.

> I was recently shown a video of a dance project that evoked some mixed and disturbing feelings. I am a NYC social worker specializing in family therapy. I was solicited for donations for a New Paltz, NY-based youth dance company, FiguresInFlight 4, collaborating with a dance company of released prisoners, FiguresInFlight-Released. The youth company is comprised of girls in their mid-teens, and the released prisoners' company is made up of men, primarily in their thirties.
>
> The prospect of young girls and older men dancing became a focus of discussions and research that raised some formidable concerns. The dance project is being marketed for funding online with a video that praises the project for giving second chances; addressing human pain/world pain; the breaking down of class and race boundaries; and the healing powers of dance. While it is possible that this project can have a positive impact, there are also issues that have not been acknowledged, most importantly, the well-being of the teenage girls.
>
> In my clinical training, it was stressed that developmentally, teenagers are at a stage that is controlled mainly through their emotions. They are exploring their sexuality and sense of self, and learning to make independent decisions. Teenage girls are easily flattered and influenced by attention from older men. This dance project places them in a highly physical situation

with older men. We need to be aware and cautious about what message this is sending to the girls in such a formative stage. My colleague who specializes in adolescent development put it well: "Given the developmental stage the girls are in, it is inappropriate. We live in a much-sexualized culture. These girls are learning to be women. They have normal sexual impulses but don't yet have the life experience to know what to do with these impulses." She further said, "Put them in a situation where they are using their bodies and dancing with adult men who have already been sexually active, and it's a combustible situation."

Dance is a physical, sensual and intimate activity. Dancers merge their emotions and bodies to create an artistic "oneness." Intense bonds are created during the many months of rehearsals that are required. Infatuations are extremely common between dance partners. With this in mind, why would a project purposely place teenage girls in a sexually charged environment with age-inappropriate partners?

Furthermore, the dances themselves have adult themes. A 2009 review of FiguresInFlight 4 in iDANZ Critix Corner stressed, 'Director Susan Slotnick brags of her students' ability to pull off modern pieces conceptualized for adults, despite being no older than your average Hannah Montana fan.'

In our culture, we try so hard to educate our youthful daughters about the parameters of proper interaction with adult men. Why is pedophilic contact okay in the context of art and dance?

At first glance, this project appears to be a positive way for the men to re-enter society. However, when I consulted people with experience in the penal system, they expressed strong disapproval. According to a doctor of sociology who is an educator and inmate/parolee advocate, 'I would never allow my daughters to participate. I would advise against doing this, given sociological and sub-cultural factors and anecdotal evidence from over 20 years with the population. I see the therapeutic and social value in expressive arts, but suggest the gender and age differences between the two groups would have a detrimental impact.' A peer counselor for prisoners, who himself was incarcerated for many years, puts it more bluntly, 'Anglos, especially who have never been imprisoned, have no idea. I am horrified that parents would permit their girls to be involved in this.'

As a former dance therapist I fully understand the benefit to the men in their own company, FiguresInFlight Released. This company has been an inspirational example of dance as a means to change lives. However, to maintain its integrity, this project must not combine the companies of young girls and older men, because it strays into and promotes pedophilia. This project is sacrificing the girls and compromising the men.

This letter is being sent to those who are involved in the project. I encourage you to pass it on.

Everyone except me received a hard copy in addition to the email. The academic tone gave the impression that it was written by a social worker, but no one with the fake name at the end was a registered social worker in New York State. I wondered if the email was a personal vendetta.

Hello Ms. Stanford,

I read with great interest your letter concerning the *Welcome to the World* project. It is clear that your concern comes from a very sincere and professional viewpoint. Probably if I did not know the people, the circumstances, and the type of choreography involved, had never volunteered with prisoners, or did not know the dancers in the youth company, I would share your concerns.

This is not the first time they have danced together. For the last four years, both groups have participated in the annual FiguresInFlight concert without incident.

The review that you quoted was from when these dancers were much younger. Another review, from a much more reputable reviewer (not a blogger) said of the same show, 'Susan Slotnick was the choreographic discovery of the Battery Dance Festival,' with no mention of the perceived inappropriateness of material. The adult theme in the dance reviewed was about creating peace first within the home.

Compared to the costumes, musical choices, and precocious movements displayed in programs like *Dance Moms*, our choreography deals with mature themes: justice, kindness, and the lack of it.

The word pedophilia is certainly frightening, but in the context of this project completely inaccurate. With knowledge of the law you would know that any man with a crime such as that has to stay away from children forever. The men of FiguresIn-Flight Released have no such history. All the parents, dancers, and men met several times in advance of going forward with the project. The choreography does not involve contact of any kind. [This was true at the time, but as trust developed within the group, we all felt that contact at the finale was not just safe but essential.]

Just as you consulted people whose opinions you valued, so did I. Even prison administrators who I talked to, who knew the men involved, supported the project wholeheartedly. We are perfor-ming at the Ethical Culture Society in New York City. The director was so impressed with the project they are cosponsoring it with a grant. Next year we have a performance at the 92nd Street Y. I appreciate your concern and I understand why, sight unseen, the idea of it could be troubling, which is why I would like to invite you to the next rehearsal to see for yourself. I have video material of the two groups; a documentary profile of me and the students from both companies has been made by Fulbright grant recipient Indrani Kopel and is available on YouTube.

I want to thank you for your interest. As dance professionals we both know the power of dance to transform lives. We live in a very stratified, classist, and racist society; many groups of people are separated. These two groups ordinarily would never know each other were it not that they are unified by the common ground of love of dance. Please feel free to call me . . . .

Questioning a project like this is important and it should be done, however, more information is needed for the criticism to be accurate.

Susan Slotnick

She never answered my email, but more unsigned letters followed. Edward Henkel, decision maker at the 92nd Street Y, told me that their policy is to disregard missives that cannot be authenticated. The performance would happen as scheduled.

I was concerned about the men. The grievous insult might cut deep into their memories of being misunderstood, presumed to be bad, unethical blobs of dangerous raging testosterone. Reluctantly I sent the email to Andre to distribute to FIF Released. They had a right to know what was being circulated about them.

From Andre:

I'm not surprised by this Susan. It was just a matter of time when someone would disregard the good in the project and look for the worst, based on their opinion and ignorance. How different is it when you and Bethany tell people that you work with prisoners. The pedophile comment was a low blow; a statement to strengthen their reasoning for disapproving the WTTW project.

Weren't some parents initially un-eased by this collaboration? They, too, must've thought the same. However, they put their trust in you.

I'm not upset about this. This was a long time coming. We just have to deal with the negative media and refocus on the project at hand.

The letter caused me to take a closer look. I asked myself the difficult questions. Was there any chance I was being naive about the men? Did I know them as well as I thought? Most had spent the years between 18 and 38 inside, looking at the permitted soft-core porn magazines and taking care of their own needs, relegated by imprison-ment to adolescent sexual behavior. All were recently released.

After so many years was it even fair to subject them to proximity with beautiful young girl dancers and keep focused on the project?

Of course they were. They were five men I worked with for many years, I know them; they are not faceless stereotypes on which suburbanites project their sexual fears. To screw up FIF Released with some tawdry, harebrained scandal would be unthinkable to them. To me they are my brothers, my sons. Let's do this. It's time to dance.

I was thankful to "Ms. Stanford" for giving me the opportunity to reexamine the project.

I was reminded of what one man said about performing inside Woodbourne. It applied perfectly to the *Welcome to the World* project.

I think the message of the performance will be clear because we all move in the same direction: we have one goal, it's the process, knowing that the process and the goal are one and the same and we are all striving to become better people.

Chapter 15

❦

Worlds Colliding

Fuckin' this, fuckin' that, and fuckin' the other thing. In prison, the f-word isn't a word but a punctuation mark, used in nearly every sentence, not just by the prisoners but the officers and staff too. An extremely cultured and polite administrator would often complain about her less efficient co-workers, "I can't deal with these fuckin' idiots anymore; I gotta get the fuck out of here!" I too often used the expletive. It had a macho feel, which, I admit, caused me to enjoy saying it.

Some dropped it when they got out. Only one man in Figuresin-Flight Released invariably salted his sentences with fuck, fuck, and more fuck. At the first rehearsal with FIF 4 and FIFR for *Welcome to the World,* he opened his mouth and out fell the word. I studied the faces of the FIF 4 members. To my relief they were not offended or shocked. They thought he was "cool." Nevertheless, I asked him to delete that word from his vocabulary at rehearsals, which he did.

Time management is a huge challenge for men recently out of prison. For decades, their time was managed for them. Even in prison, when they were responsible for getting somewhere on their own, they would often be late or not show up at all. This was a constant irritation in the dance program, since if a man was late the officer would not allow him into the dance space.

Casper (Christian Plant), recently released, had a difficult time getting to the first WTTW rehearsal. He missed his train, then realized he was short a few dollars to purchase a ticket from Yonkers to Poughkeepsie, where my husband waited to pick him up and bring him to

187

the dance studio. I was so desperate to get him there that I actually told him to beg for money in the train station. My suggestion was beneath his dignity. He went to a relative's house and borrowed the money.

Six-foot-three, skinny, agile, extraordinarily good-looking, with high cheekbones, neatly braided hair, and a face that is the epitome of symmetry, Casper entered the studio late. The kids could hardly keep from staring at his imposing presence. Having everyone's attention caused him a little anxiety, but he quickly overcame it when he saw his compatriots from Woodbourne. "I felt like I was home," he told me.

Casper grew up in Yonkers. He did well academically in his freshman year of high school. In spite of that, as soon as he turned sixteen, he quit high school and began to sell drugs. When the street life took over he lost all his aspirations. He doesn't remember ever wanting to be something when he grew up, since he didn't expect to live past the age of twenty-one. He was incarcerated at sixteen, let out at eighteen; within months he was rearrested, charged, and sentenced. By the time I met him he was thirty.

What turned him around was becoming an inspiration to his little cousin who was locked up in the same facility. Up to that point Casper hadn't made the commitment to change. On the street he'd been a bad influence on his younger cousin, so he blamed himself for the boy's fate.

In 2007 Casper had been accepted to the highly competitive, prestigious Bard College prison program which would allow him to attain a college degree while imprisoned. Right after his acceptance, he was "keep-locked" for one hundred twenty days. Keep-lock is a lesser form of punishment than solitary confinement: prisoners are kept in their own dormitory or cell, but lose privileges like commissary, phone calls, packages, and all programs. His acceptance to Bard would be rescinded if he missed classes again. It all came together; change crystallized in Casper, and he left his old ways behind.

Ali Cindell Kelly began dancing after he saw FiguresInFlight 5 perform a dance entitled, *Be Grateful*. In prison Ali made his mark by becoming a master at crochet: toys, hats, scarves, even delicate necklaces. He made dozens of tiny colorful hats in the style of Muslim prayer caps and sent them to hospitals for preemies to wear in neonatal units.

On the morning of Ali's release, he came straight to my house for a celebration breakfast. Joann Still, his music teacher, Shawn Fisher, his theater teacher, his poetry teacher, and his daughter all came to join us, we watched him take his first few steps as a free man, up my driveway. Out of a big bag emerged crocheted presents for everyone. Sam got a scarf and headband in the colors of the Minnesota Vikings, Ali's favorite football team.

Although he quit the dance program a year before his release, Ali rejoined and became part of the WTTW project. During the first rehearsal he was confident, mayoral in style, always smiling. To me, he shared his concerns. Had the kids Googled him? Did they know about his crime? Had I told the parents? He was worried about the letter opposing the project, and he wondered how many other naysayers were out there, but that first rehearsal had been powerful.

"It only took ten minutes and I was comfortable, like I never left dance. At first, I felt like the kid in the corner, but everyone welcomed me into the fold, into the family, and the child in the corner was back in the circle with everyone else!"

Over the years I'd shown videos of FIF 4 in the prison, and on some level Ali felt as though he knew the FIF dancers already. He called Liam Appelson "little brother." When I told everyone they had to put away their cell phones, Ali had a pro tip for the dancers. "I'm not wearing tights so I can hide my cell phone from Susan in my sweatpants pocket." Immediately, there was common ground.

Ali grew up in Brooklyn, an average student and an exceptional football player. During his junior year he received two or three letters a week from colleges and universities offering him football scholarships if he met the academic requirements. Ali's English teacher was openly bisexual, and Ali was raised to disapprove, so he stopped going to class. Failing English and sustaining a knee injury doomed his prospects and began his spiral into the street life. He was a runner, the person who takes the drugs from the supplier, gives them to the user, gets the money and runs back to the dealer. He made a small fortune at a young age, which attracted the jealousy of the older drug traffickers and put his life in danger. At fifteen he was arrested and spent two weeks at Rikers Island juvenile facility.

At sixteen, he married his sweetheart in a Sunni Muslim ceremony. The marriage was a religious commitment, with no legal standing. Ali, in any case, wasn't ready for lifelong monogamy. He fathered a daughter with another girl.

At eighteen, Ali committed a violent crime and received twenty years to life. Two and a half years of his sentence were spent in solitary confinement. After seven years he received a letter from the mother of his victim, comparing his life to the life her son might have had if he was not murdered. Victim and perpetrator corresponded for the next seven years. She forgave him. That event, and his shame when his mother and daughter saw him chained and shackled during a visit, supplied the impetus for change. He vowed to stay out of trouble, and never let his daughter see him chained and shackled again. He also was accepted to the prestigious Bard college prison program.

Many years before I went into a prison to teach dance, I'd choreographed a ten-minute dance to Nina Simone's jazz version of "Sinnerman," for Bethany's company, FiguresInFlight 2. The steps were appropriate for young, fully-trained dancers, but the theme of sin and redemption was a peculiar choice for young kids whose greatest crimes were probably refusing to clean their rooms. The blogger reviewer would no doubt, disapprove.

Bethany and I decided to restage it at Woodbourne. I suggested that we simplify the choreography, but she refused. "We're going to teach it step for step and make it happen," she said. Bethany added weekly rehearsals.

In the original pieces three-foot-long sticks were needed for a rhythm section. The correct word to use here, to describe what Bethany had to do, is *schlepped*; Yiddish for an arduous journey or procedure, to "carry or drag" something difficult. Every rehearsal Bethany schlepped thirty sticks, waited while each one was X-rayed, then fumbled carrying them through the prison to the dance space. *Sinnerman* was a favorite dance; by far the most complex and technical out of the dozens of dances choreographed over the years.

One dancer put hours, weeks and months into forcing his forty-one-year-old body to twist, turn, jump, and count the complicated combinations in *Sinnerman*, only to miss the opportunity to perform it with the other men because of a sudden transfer in preparation for release.

"I joined the dance program to regain the sense of humanity I lost during my twenty years locked up, almost half of my life. Dance is a statement from the soul, I get to be and be seen for who I really am. I saw it as an opportunity to dismantle the walls I built up around myself. I was afraid to dance, so logically I knew if I did, it would give me courage to conquer my fears," he said.

Dancing with the "professionals," FIF 4, made one dancer nervous at first. Could he measure up? He was surprised by how open, accepting, and comfortable the students were with him. When Cady Kristal approached him during a short break and offered to help him with the steps, he was touched by her kindness. Partly fueled by remorse for his errors, partly just because of the guy he is, he had a huge drive to pay back kindness. First, he offered the students free tickets to a Jets football game. Then he had stylish FiguresInFlight Released t-shirts made for all the dancers.

At first, I objected. Knowing the financial struggle, the men when released, I assumed it must be a hardship for him to give us gifts, but it came from the heart.

Luis Diaz, nicknamed Flex, would stand at the gate waiting for the bell to ring announcing "movement" to prison programs and dash to the dance space. He was always the first one in the room, every Sunday for six years, never once missing class for illness or a visit from home. Dance, he said, was his "life-altering passion." "I practice in the mess hall or a corner of the gymnasium, practicing steps over and over, without shame or self-consciousness, I love it."

Bethany and I were his family, his only Sunday visitors.

Flex had stopped going to school in the fifth grade. Paying attention was difficult and the streets called to him. His father was a kingpin, an important gangster and drug lord, with 1000 people at his command. Dealing drugs was the family business. At ten years old Flex joined his mother and father selling heroin on the streets of the Lower East Side.

"I loved the streets," he told me. "They were my escape from the dullness of school. The streets were gritty, musical, with a drum beat undercurrent of excitement and sound. I was a twelve-year-old kid the first time I got arrested. They sent me away to Sugarloaf Youth Prison for one year. Then I was back to selling heroin again. By this time my father was in prison, so I was needed to support my mother and brother."

In 1985, at fifteen, Flex was rearrested for dealing drugs. This time he served eighteen months at Highland Correctional Facility, where I first taught prisoners. At seventeen he was arrested for the third time, again for selling heroin, and sent to Rikers Island. When he turned eighteen, he was locked up with the adults.

"Rikers was a terrible, frightening place. COs were beating up guys, people were cutting each other. There were constant, violent fights. I intervened when a group tried to molest a young kid. For that I was sent to solitary for sixty days, along with the kid and the people trying to hurt him."

After being released from Rikers, Flex went to live with his grandmother. Though she lived in the same neighborhood, he hoped that her calmer apartment would be a fortress where he could resist easy money and fast times. Some things went well: he fell in love with a girl named Brunilda, and they lived together. He got a job in a Crab House and tried to straighten out and stay focused.

He remembers it as a happy time. It wasn't enough, and his old ways began to creep back in and soon he was in trouble. He caught another drug charge, and this time was sent away for two years. Released again, he fell in love with a woman named Pitaina and had a baby girl named Maria. But Flex was still a creature of the streets. He ran around, sold drugs; it was only a matter of time before disaster struck. During a fight he hurt someone. This time he was given a straight bid, fifteen years, with no opportunities for early release through parole.

Five years into his sentence, while at Sing Sing, Flex discovered Rehabilitation Through the Arts. He was cast in a production of West Side Story, given the part of Chino, a member of the Puerto Rican Jets gang. He began to study Shakespeare, Macbeth in particular. He needed to learn to cooperate, communicate, and get along with others, and the RTA theater program provided that opportunity.

When Flex got transferred to Woodbourne, he happened to pass by the room where we were rehearsing and decided to join the dance program. His style of dancing was ballistic, strong, but a bit choppy. We worked together to smooth out, connect the movements and increase his emotional range.

We also worked on the whole issue of self-evaluation. During the philosophy section of class, Flex announced that he had no skills. It was shocking, sad, and inaccurate. Evaluating himself was a skill Flex needed to acquire; sometimes he didn't know how good he was, other times he didn't know his deficits.

Then one Sunday Flex wasn't there. Another dancer nonchalantly told me he'd been transferred. He was the first man but not the last to suddenly disappear. I felt robbed of that particular virtue and joy, of teaching such a gifted and eager learner, with even the chance to say goodbye. That's prison life; hard to plan for, impossible to control, and very hard to bear.

After his release, Flex called me. He wanted to continue dancing. Andre invited him to join FIFR, and I asked him to participate in the WTTW project. Flex, who was never late, almost missed the first WTTW rehearsal. Navigating time, as a free man in the big society, was so often a problem, and so was meeting a troupe of suburban school kids. "I felt strange, apprehensive, I didn't know how I'd be received, how to interact with the young dancers. I wanted to be on my best behavior, but I wasn't sure what that was supposed to be. Be myself? Who was I in a situation so unfamiliar? But as soon as I saw Bethany, she was like an angel to me, and I felt calm. It was my first time seeing her as a free man."

In the ending of *Welcome to the World,* each person is lifted above the rest and slowly brought down into a compassionate embrace. Flex was frightened. Because of his position in the clump he was required to hug Solo Masson–Diedhiou, a ten-year-old girl.

Flex describes the moment in Indrani's film. "I was reminded of the last time I hugged my daughter. That was fourteen years ago. Holding Solo reminded me of the mistake I made which put me in the position not to be a father to my daughter. (Flex is tearing up, his voice quivering. One of the men puts an arm around his shoulder) It's kind of ...I'm trying to find the right words...it threw me off for a minute because, you know, it's been a long time since I hugged a child...just now was actually the first time in fourteen years that I actually hugged a child. It scared me because when you see a newborn baby for the first time, you don't know how to handle it, you hesitate a little. And that's how I felt (another arm goes around his shoulder) and I didn't want to say nothing because I didn't want to cry. That's just pride getting in the way... I'm glad I had the opportunity today to hug a child."

The camera pans over to Kristen, Solo's mother, who is also crying.

One of the FIF Released dancers, whose name I am withholding, didn't do well in school. Judging from his achievements in later life, he simply wasn't challenged. To amuse himself and assuage his boredom, he "majored in clowning and minored in bullying."

His parents separated when he was five years old, his father stayed involved. He was charming and popular, and the older tough kids in the neighborhood began to notice him. He often hung out after school in the public library, not because he liked to read but because it was where the pretty girls he knew spent time. In fifth grade, he started to cut school. He'd take his lunch money, go to the corner candy store, and play arcade games until he ran out of quarters. For the remainder of the day he sat on a bench in the park, "bored out of his mind."

One afternoon his grandfather happened by during school hours and found him swinging on a tire. His grandfather "whooped" him for the entire three blocks home. His old-country Mexican grandparents were much stricter than his parents. That was the first and last time he received a beating from his grandfather, but it made an impression, and he tried to get interested in school.

It didn't last. In ninth grade, he quit and joined a gang. At first the activities of the Graffiti Bombing Kings were just graffiti and minor vandalism. At first, he wasn't a violent kid; he admired the fly girls, break dancers, and graffiti artists, not the fighters.

As he grew more at home on the street, he became intrigued by the power and respect the tough kids who committed more serious crimes received from their peers. He started joining in, receiving popularity and respect from all the wrong people. At sixteen, he was sitting in a car outside while his friends were robbing a store. A man was killed, and everyone was charged with felony murder regardless of the level of their participation.

He was convicted and sent to Rikers Island, then upstate to Elmira where he spent thirty days in solitary confinement. He read the biography of Malcolm X and vowed to emulate him by getting a GED and going on to college.

Unfortunately for him and tens of thousands of others, Governor Pataki delivered a crushing blow to inmate higher education. College programs disappeared overnight. Instead of attending school, prisoners sat idle under a miasma of dashed dreams and hopelessness. His aspirations foiled, he relapsed into hanging out in the yard and getting involved in gang activity.

Ten years into his incarceration a phone call from his mother inspired him to change. She let him have it over the phone; their bond still mattered very much to him. The phone call was a turning point. He stepped away from the gang life, determined this time to get an education, and requested a transfer south to be closer to his family. He graduated from the GED program, and eventually found his way to Woodbourne.

He was invited to participate in an eight-week introduction-to-college program by a panel of his peers, a huge honor. This led to his acceptance to the Bard College Prison Initiative, where he earned his associate's degree. When he started college, he was already in the dance program. I attended his graduation on a beautiful spring day, the prison yard transformed for the event. Under a vast, billowing white tent were classical musicians from Bard College, epicurean food, along with a procession of men in caps and gowns. Mothers, fathers, sons, daughters and wives watched as their loved ones received college degrees. For some families that was the proudest moment ever with their sons whose lives, until then, brought more sorrow than joy.

"I was on a path toward self-discovery,"

"If something was beautiful, intimidating, and beneficial, it called to me. I joined the dance program out of curiosity. I heard this beautiful music by Ryuichi Sakamoto, and it hit me at my emotional core. Something told me to get up and try it; I wasn't at ease just watching. When I danced, I felt myself in a new way, from my gut, not from my head. It filled me with love, passion, and compassion. Dance allowed me to experience emotions for which there are no words, righteousness of spirit, joy, pain, and sadness simultaneously."

Shortly after his release he reconnected with his high school sweetheart. Soon her pregnancy dominated his thoughts. He wanted more than anything to be a daddy. "I spent twenty years in prison, from seventeen to thirty-seven supposedly the best years of my life, and had only one real regret. I wanted a child. When I got out I didn't chase women, or the crazy dreams a lot of the guys have: build an empire, make lots of money. All I wanted was to live my freedom as an adult, struggle with the daily grind and be independent. I did everything right, lived on my own, got a job, and anxiously awaited the birth.

"I was thrust into the dance piece. Ironically, *Welcome to The World* mirrored where I was in my life. The piece is about conflict and compassion. Someone watching might only perceive one of those two aspects, but seeing both, containing at once the tension of opposites, is what the dance is about. At the end of rehearsal when we formed a circle and were asked for feedback, I didn't want to speak at first, but then the spirit moved me. I talked about the ending, when one at a time, dancers are lifted, lowered and hugged. Fatherhood was always on my mind, so I spoke about how the first second of life is just like the ending of the dance: we are lifted out of the womb and hugged.

"You came up to me and told me that a few of the girls wanted the film of my words sent to them. That gave me confidence. Daily life moves so fast, all my communications are functional, you know? 'Pass the salt.' 'What time are you coming home?' That type of thing. Rehearsal was when I could relax, let my guard down, communicate on a really human level, and speak from my heart. You refer to FiguresIn-Flight 1,2,3,4, and FiguresInFlight Released with different acronyms, but to me it's just one community FiguresInFlight Dance Company; all of us, family, no difference, all coming from one root."

After the letter from "Ms. Stanford," he shared his reaction. "She has had a negative effect on me, I admit it. I feel self-conscious, I am watching my every move, worried about where to put my hands when I help lift a dancer up at the end of the piece."

After a lifetime of wishing, his dream came true. His daughter was born on May 5th, premature, weighing one pound twelve ounces after only twenty-five weeks' gestation. His reason to live, his job, his passion, became centered on the tiny baby, nestled into the neonatal unit at New York-Presbyterian Hospital.

Whenever the infant heard her father's voice she would raise her little arm in his direction. Muffled as the sound was through the incubator, the baby reached toward her father every time.

I tried to keep my concerns about the little child to myself. My worries were assuaged by one delightful visit when the baby was finally home, thriving, looking chubbier, an exquisitely formed little baby-girl all pink and tan.

I received a call the morning after Thanksgiving 2014 and was told the child had died.

Later that afternoon, I picked up a message left early that morning. "Hello, Susan. I have something to tell you, I don't want you to hear it from anyone else but me." What had I done to receive the privilege of that call? I was humbled by his concern at this darkest moment of his new life. So much love between all of us, so much trust in spite of the Ms. Stanford's of the world who'll never understand the bond we've built.

He was the designated spokesperson of FiguresInFlight Released. He struggled during Q & A session to describe his frame of mind since his child died.

I am so angry. She didn't have to die. She was fine, doubled her weight, She worked so hard to survive. Then she had a fever for three days, and we begged the doctors at this big-deal hospital to just give her a test for bacterial pneumonia. They kept insisting it was viral. Those doctors. They didn't care. By the time they administered the test it was too late. The antibiotic didn't work, and she was gone. It was so preventable.

People are asking us if we're going to sue. I am not a socialist, but dammit, capitalism… in this society a baby isn't worth much. A baby doesn't bring in income. We just want the doctors never to do this to another family again. I spent 20 years in prison. I'm an ex-convict. Did they think I was less human? What if it was the doctor's baby?

I have no words to describe the love, joy, and compassion I learned during my child's seven months of life. I didn't know feelings that huge were possible in this world. Every second was worth it. If I had to, I would go back to prison for another twenty years just to taste that again.

A lot has changed, I feel very different: angry, disappointed, and helpless. Hours go by and I am lost in my thoughts, in introspection. That's all I do now, just think, and try to understand. Yet somehow, through it all, even with this anger, I would never hurt anyone. My daughter's dad doesn't do things like that. I don't do things like that. I still believe in myself.

Throughout the spring, the lead-up to our recital had the usual logistical glitches in getting everyone upstate, and the long greetings among the men always made me want to shriek, "Get on with it, time's being wasted!" But the next three rehearsals intensified the deeply celebratory, hard-working connection we were building between the two groups. Twelve young FIF4 dancers, five FIF Released men, Molly Rust, Elianah Slotnick, Jonathan Villegas, Jared Wootan, and I all contributed, making Welcome to The World come alive again; dozens of cooks, each with a necessary spice, all of us sharing laughter, poignancy, excitement and love. We knew we were doing something special. Tiny, blond, adorable Cali Krishner, deep in a first-position plié beside big brown rotund Ali Cindell Kelly, also in a plié, made an unforgettable optic, something that might never have been seen in the world and probably never would again.

After dancing for a few hours, it was time to feast. There is nothing like a long table of delicious food when one is hungry from hours of dancing. The FIF 4 dancers each cooked a dish, and I brought a four-foot-long hero sandwich. Bodies love to eat, hearts communicate over food, smells and sights stimulate the brain. There they were ex-prisoners and country kids, sharing what felt like a holiday meal.

No matter how prepared I tried to be, even after twenty years, concert day was always grueling. June 7th, 2014 dawned perfect and sunny: 80 degrees, clear, low humidity. Inside McKenna Theatre, it was dark, humid, and dank; the air conditioning system was broken, and no one from the college seemed even interested in fixing it. The dancers gathered in mid-morning to begin the unrelenting, sweaty drudgery of technical rehearsal, when music and lighting cues are nailed down while the dancers stood around waiting, fanning themselves.

The temperature in the theatre was steadily inching up past 90 degrees, like a giant soggy blanket spread over our aspirations and raw nerves. It's always stressful waiting to see if we get a big audience. Every year I get tense, convinced that this is the year no one will come, afraid that the feast one year in the making will be laid out at an empty table. I stared into the parking lot and counted cars. This concert, bringing the two companies together to perform *Welcome to the World*, one year from retirement, was the most important of all the concerts.

I was afraid half the audience would turn and leave when they realized how hot and stuffy the theater would become during the two-hour performance. What would happen once three hundred hot bodies were crowded into the already unendurable space? At the last minute, we purchased three hundred bottles of water and handed them out along with the tickets.

I hoped to sit back, in a cool place, and watch my choreography in the privacy of my own mind. So frightened was I that an exodus would occur after each piece, I was compelled to emcee the entire performance with my impromptu standup routine. "Welcome to the FiguresInFlight sweat lodge," I said. The lights came on, the music began. People stayed, and so it goes.

Chapter 16

∞∾

Renewal

I ndrani completed her seventeen-minute profile thus:

Scene one: I am riding in my car after picking up Indrani at the bus top.

"I've done a lot of things in my life, I've painted a lot of pictures, I've written a lot of articles, I have choreographed over a thousand dances. [I thought I might have exaggerated this until I counted. Approximately 1100 residency dances, another 200 for my youth companies, and another 35 in the prisons.], but somehow when I walk into this room in the prison, I get the overwhelming feeling that everything I have ever done in my life was a step towards that room."

Indrani ends the film with a quote from one of the formerly incarcerated dancers.

"She comes into a prison environment, an environment where, honestly, the message is you're not much if you are anything at all, and she says, 'No, I think you're the world, I think you are the cream of the crop, I don't think those out there are the cream of the crop. I think you in here are, and I challenge you to start seeing yourself in that fashion, and let's see what happens.' Thus, I call her the game changer."

That was the title Indrani chose, *The Game Changer*. It was accepted into 16 film festivals, receiving first prize for best documentary at the Harlem International Film Festival and first prize at the Cannes Film Festival for emerging filmmakers (American Pavilion). Sam and I followed the film from festival to festival, enjoying sitting in the dark with strangers, watching ourselves on the big screen.

In between the beginning and the ending quote among many other scenes, I can be seen furiously and aerobically raking leaves, trying to elevate my pulse, and ferociously and aerobically working out in my studio, trying to burn some calories. Did I mind hundreds of people seeing me in the act of being myself? Not at all.

Sam is filmed making carrot juice. We decided that the carrot juice scene was our favorite.

Close-up of Sam's hands washing carrots.

Voiceover (Sam):

"Susan's a creative person, and she has angels and she has demons; I think that's the source of her creativity. I know she came from a very wounded childhood, and that requires a tremendous amount of healing."

Cut to Sam holding a beautifully prepared plate of organic carrots, celery, kale and apples.

"Sometimes we make beet green and cucumber juice. It's easier to prepare if you hold with the blade rather than the handle." He shows me the plate and says, referring to Indrani's inquiry, "She asked if I do this for you."

"No." I say, "It's for the both of us. We do it every day."

In each theater, at each festival, Sam and I held hands during the carrot juice scene and tried to muffle our laughter. Was it possible this was interesting to complete strangers? It seemed so, from the applause. A husband in the kitchen providing healthy juice for his wife... the wife madly raking leaves.

We traveled across country to Portland chasing *The Game Changer*. The level of mellowness in the City of Roses was so extreme it appeared the entire population was competing for a mad chill award. The film was supposed to be screened four times, but wound up being shown only twice. The festival was disorganized; some filmmakers traveled halfway around the world and their films were never shown. Equipment problems and scheduling mistakes did not faze the festival's director, whose stock response to complaints was, "Oh well,"

I ordered a goat cheese pizza in an overpriced eatery, specifying that I was allergic to cow's milk. "Oh well," the waitress said.

There was a lot of anger lurking under the veneer of "mad chill." Passive aggression seemed to be a Portland civic duty.

Marijuana became legal in Oregon for the first time while we were there. The last time we'd bought cannabis had been forty-five years earlier in Morocco. We looked up marijuana dispensaries in the yellow pages and called around, only to be told we had to be full-time residents of Oregon. "Oh well, sorry, we don't want an influx of thousands of out-of-state people flocking here to get high." We hadn't really wanted the stuff anyway. Just the novel experience of purchasing it legally. We walked around the unfamiliar streets, looking in store windows, passing hundreds of travelers, mostly young people who migrate up the coast from California during summer.

The last time Sam and I traveled together to a new place without our daughters had been our youthful journey around the world as newlyweds. We'd hardly known each other or ourselves, we had no idea of the road ahead. Forty-five years later, we had only five more to go to make it to our 50th wedding anniversary.

During the Q & A after a screening, ten young filmmakers just starting out were invited on stage to answer a pass-along question.

"What are your future aspirations?" Each young artist outlined their next big project. When it was my turn, I said, "I want to make it to my 50th wedding anniversary. Staying married that long requires massive creative energy."

In Portland Sam and I renewed our devotion in a rarefied space that too few married couples are lucky enough to experience. We've pulled through so many adversities, another entire book's worth; heartaches too numerous and deep to remember. There is a litany of sins, like the "Al Chet" prayer that we say many times during the Yom Kippur service; we have our own list of mistakes, sins, betrayals, selfishness, dishonesty, and hardened spots in our hearts. But on that trip, in Portland, we realized that we've accomplished our own marital *teshuva*, or turning around. We caught all the falls in time and shifted directions.

Our marriage will never look romantic to our daughters, who see all the little daily irritations, but seeing Sam age, reflecting my own advancing years, is sobering. He was a boy of thirteen and I was a girl of eleven the summer we met at the Beach and Tennis Club in New Rochelle. Now a seventy-one-year-old man lies beside a sixty-nine-year-old woman.

The sweet man my mother forced me into marrying, and I, came to see ourselves and each other in a new way. The time together in Portland, the city of "Oh well," became a second honeymoon, a gift brought to us as an indirect result of the prison dance program.

Chapter 17

Long Goodbyes

In September 2014, I began my final year of teaching, choreographing, mounting performances, and passing on whatever wisdom I accrued to young people. Public education in America has all but deleted the fine and performing arts from the curriculum; this despite the work of renowned educational and brain researcher Dr. Robert Sylwester, who concluded at the end of an exhaustive lifelong inquiry that arts should be the core curriculum. Children pay attention to what has emotional significance more deeply than what just stimulates the intellect. The arts were slowly being eliminated and artist residencies became even rarer.

Teaching students to pay attention using dance, my spur-of-the-moment invention, had a great run: at least 10,000 students have been through the program, and hundreds of teachers and parents have used the concepts in their own endeavors. Once I had sixty days a year of residencies in schools. In this last year, it has dwindled to thirteen. But the impact on the students who did take part continued to increase.

Newcomb Central School teacher Martha Swan is a hold-out, believing that character education, arts, and life skills are as important as math and reading. She hired me to teach the entire school. Nestled in a remote section of the Adirondacks, Newcomb is the smallest district in New York, with just one hundred students in pre-k through twelfth grades. Although this residency would prove to be one of the last, still the reaction was as intense as the first residency decades ago in Ellenville.

Dear Susan and Bethany,

Thank you so much for coming to our school to teach us to dance—it was an amazing experience. It's crazy to discover the things us teenagers are blind to until people like you come and point it out. When we did the show dancing with a partner and you talked about how eye contact is rare now, I noticed you were totally right—although I had never thought about it. Also, when you were talking about how we rely on our friends decisions/ opinions to form our own—it sadly is completely true! I really enjoyed the documentary you showed us too, because it shows you can't judge someone on a mistake they made for the rest of their life. I would never imagine seeing men in prison expressing their emotions and dancing like they did in the video—but it was breath-taking. Thank you again for such a once in a life time experience.

With love and attention,
(Since you can't love something without
first directing your attention to it!)

On Armistice Day 2015 I turned seventy years old. All I had left was the prison dance program and FiguresinFlight 4. After thirty-seven years, FiguresInFlight would end in four short months. Four times now, over thirty-seven years, I've loved, mentored, and trained groups from five years old to the brink of adulthood. Now FiguresinFlight students were applying for college and preparing to leave home.

There were difficult and wonderful times with FIF4's students. As they were on the precipice of leaving they took a downward turn and some became smug and disrespectful. I would often leave the studio heavy-hearted, walking to my car in the cold, winter night, wondering whether I was too old. Was ageism causing them to marginalize me?

Hints of scorn and judgment, as well as smirking glances, were exchanged when I said a wrong word, taught a sequence too fast, or was unclear. This polluted the room and triggered feelings in me reminiscent of high school. These are the smart kids: popular, pretty, and clean. I didn't fit with them. I did not know how to be with these students; it was disquieting in the final days.

"Movie night" had always been a FiguresInFlight tradition. At Christmastime, the dancers and I watched *A Christmas Carol* or *It's a Wonderful Life*; both films each for their huge philosophical ideas offered without a shred of pretension: salvation through self-knowledge, the effect on the world of one individual's deeds.

The class was treating me as if I didn't know what I was doing. Under their scorn, I became self-conscious and uncomfortable; I started dreading my time with them, wishing I could retire right away. Molly Rust also noticed, which was helpful since I was afraid I was imagining or overreacting. After a few days of contemplation, I decided to cancel movie night.

At the next class, I told them not to get into their dance clothes. They were the best technicians, I told them, and if that was what mattered most, I'd have had no problem. But technique was secondary. I delivered a "philosophy class" during which, to my dismay, I started to cry. I believe in the importance of vulnerability. It often feels like weakness but actually it's the opposite; it takes courage to reveal yourself, especially in public, with people who might not have your best interests at heart. But that brave philosophy can be hard to remember when you find yourself tearing up in front of a group of teenagers.

Liam had just been accepted to Yale. He'll be starting when he is seventeen. I decided to use him as my example.

Yale students are engaged in various projects connected to the criminal justice system, workshops, tutoring, GED preparation, mentoring projects, and discussion groups as well as broader social justice projects related to prison reform. The college is very proud of their prison initiatives. Out of the thousands of applications received for the class of 2015, it can be assumed that Liam's was the only one reflecting that he'd already worked with prisoners on the social justice project, *Welcome to the World*.

I suggested that might have given him an edge. He nodded in agreement. "So behind you are all the men in FiguresInFlight Released who helped get you into Yale, also your teachers and your parents. Behind them are all the people who helped them become who they are. Behind them are more people. No one gets into college or succeeds in life alone. There are hundreds of people behind you and you owe them humility, and gratitude. And especially respect.

I asked the other students to visualize all the people standing behind them. Thanking is not enough. It's how you use what has been given to you that will show your gratitude.

I asked them to identify what needed improvement in their behavior.

Liam said he wanted to be more helpful and less scornful of his peers. Did he automatically think he would be once he was a Yale? He nodded. You need to start now, I told him. One becomes what is practiced; behavior doesn't change from changing locations.

Just a few weeks earlier I'd finally gotten the students to stay off their phones in the studio. Their inability to be present, the constant necessity to amuse themselves with social media, seemed to morph them into mechanized creatures unable to speak openly, make eye contact, share thoughts and feelings without hiding behind devices. One can only pay attention to one thing at a time, and all though class their attention was diverted. They missed so much of what was going on around them. Observing other people is important. Wisdom and insight comes from being present and watchful.

After I cancelled movie night and banned phones, the change was miraculous. Challenged, they rose.

I was stunned by Cady's and River's college entrance essays. Cady usually spoke in qualifiers, often taking back her words as swiftly as she spoke them. "Never mind, I don't know, sort of, maybe, kind of, I'm not sure," punctuated much of her oral communication.

River was known within the company for lighthearted banter, and appeared unconcerned about her size. I knew from my own experience that not having a typical dancer's body was painful. When she asked me to suggest a topic for her college essay I suggested she write about being an atypical dancer among the skinny girls.

Both essays confirmed that these two internalized the philosophy. I am and will always be so proud of them.

Untitled
by River Wasser

My heart races as I step forward; our eyes lock and for a moment, we remain synchronized. I am staring into his huge, brown eyes, and for a moment, they are not eyes, but windows. Through these windows, I recognize pain, and for this moment, we are the same. For as long as I have been a member of FiguresInFlight dance company, my dance teacher has instructed a dance program inside the walls of a medium-security men's prison. The program serves as a method of rehabilitation by encouraging expression through movement. Men who are stereotyped as cold-hearted and aggressive dance with power and emotion. Many men who went through the program have claimed that dance has altered the paths of their lives and even

choose to continue dancing after release. When I was a sophomore in high school, I was given the opportunity to collaborate
with these released men to perform a dance entitled "Welcome
to the World." Countless weekends were spent sharing a common rehearsal space, telling stories, and getting to know each
other. Our time together left me with an unanswered question:
what allowed us to develop a deep understanding and acceptance of each other with the awareness that we had so little in
common? Our differences seemed ubiquitous: I was a 14-year-
old White girl who grew up with stability, while they were middle-aged African American ex-convicts All I knew was that we
were two completely different groups of people, united through
movement. I have always been bigger and taller than all of my
peers. At first glance, my size would belie any idea of me being
a dancer. My dance company is comprised of girls who are perfect in my eyes: toned, skinny, and flexible. I have always felt
huge in comparison. It takes a tremendous amount of courage
to get up on stage and focus on my performance rather than
my appearance, but I don't allow my weight to set me back. I
dance with passion and empathy because moving makes me
feel beautiful and provides me with an outlet for my emotions.
Despite my determination, I have always felt different because
I am different. Although I work to combat my challenges, I
cannot ignore the isolation I feel from being overweight. My
feelings of hurt helped me recognize what I had in common
with these previously incarcerated men: they have felt this pain
too. These men have endured intangible hardships yet dance
powerfully to heal themselves, despite the fact that prisoners,
let alone grown men, are not expected to dance. I discovered
a bond that plunged deeper than our connection through
dance: our connection through pain. My introduction to the
released men allowed me to find a common link with people

who seemed completely different from me. I realize that we are both outsiders, people who aren't naturally talented dancers. We don't fit the mold, but we dance anyway. Although the pain and isolation we feel comes from different experiences, we still share a common pain. Our shared pain is what fostered our source of compassion, understanding, and connection. In this colliding of two seemingly separate worlds' I have realized that although in some ways we could not be more different, our desire for healing makes us fundamentally the same. I find comfort knowing that this experience encouraged me to find a connection with the outcasts of society, the commonly misunderstood. I have learned that beneath the surface, all human beings share this linkage of brokenness. This brokenness is what bonds us together. Some of us are fractured by the choices we make, some by our lack of self-confidence, and some by the heartbreak that we are unable to control, but our shared pain is the basis for our search for human understanding. We are all not so different after all.

Thirty-Two Counts
by Cady Kristal-Cohen

I could feel the gnarly floor pressing against my sweaty palms. The percussive beat of the music repeatedly smacked against my forehead. The symphony of jumping feet moved in a frenzied unison behind me, taunting me to join. My heart races as the music reaches a crescendo, my cue to stand. I rise and turn to my left reaching out my hand. My partner is waiting, just as we've practiced. We stand a foot apart, facing each other, completely motionless and for a moment, there is clarity. My heart slows. For exactly thirty-two seconds, ticked off automatically in my head, I do not think. I do not falter. I forget the bodies moving upstage, the rapid-fire thoughts and the pressure. I forget my feet on the floor and the itch in my leotard. All that's left, in those thirty-two counts, on that stage, in the heart of New York City is the truth. A hundred eyes observed us from their seats, but the moment was solely contained between my partner and I. The response was automatic and simultaneously overwhelming, triggered by the rarity of unfaltering eye contact. Reflected in Joconia's eyes, I saw unfiltered human pain, a desire to be loved and breath-taking vulnerability. I found myself revealing, to a man I barely knew, emotions that I'd only let peek out in the darkness of my bedroom. I could feel past heartbreaks and betrayals spilling up and out and over, messily slung onto the stage floor. It was truthfully terrifying, yet somehow beneath the fear, gratifying to feel something and see it so wholly reflected by another. In that moment, it became clear that at the most primitive level of human emotions, we were explicably the same. That was the most profound and uncomp-licated truth that I have ever or potentially will ever know.

The man that stands before me is African American and aggressively tall, while I am light-skinned and slight. He is in his mid-thirties, while I have yet to qualify as an adult. He was born into the ghetto of Yonkers, while I was born into middle class suburbia. I spent the last seventeen years of my life growing up conventionally, he had spent the past seventeen years behind bars for manslaughter in the first degree. Without these seemingly vast differences, my realization that we were fundamentally the same wouldn't have been nearly as personally revolutionary. For that, I am forever grateful for that man, that night on the stage and the opportunity that brought me there. For as long as I have been a member of the professional youth dance company FiguresInFlight, roughly twelve years, my teacher has taught inside the prison walls of the Woodbourne Correctional Facility every Sunday, religiously. As we grew older, a handful of men were released and formed their own company, dedicated to preventing incarceration for children at risk. While we usually perform separately, we were recently given the opportunity to collaborate. After dancing with these men, my preconceived notions of a prisoner have been shattered and replaced with a sense of humility. Yes, these men did make a felonious mistake, but they are so much more than their past lifestyle or decisions. They are their vulnerability, their pain and their loneliness. They have taught me that on a fundamental level, all humans seek love and acceptance. We are all confined by our own varied, yet equally honorable battles of vulnerability, pain and loneliness. Since that night, I've kept that morsel of truth firmly cupped between my small palms and I intend to approach every situation and every individual with the same sense of equality and openness that I was handed to me in those thirty-two counts, on that stage, in the heart of New York City.

Chapter 18

———— ✦ ————

Very Wounded People, All of Us

A prison is like a monastery with captive participants, or a rehab with opportunities for spiritual growth and religious observance in a mostly drug-free environment without distractions. Although the men are working on becoming their best selves, they are still wounded people. Locked up for decades, sometimes treated harshly by staff, many coming from inner city poverty and lack of opportunity, they struggle to function as mature adults.

Inside, they have big wishes for themselves. Since every minute of every day, week, month, year, and decade they live with the constant reminder of their misdeeds, remorse is a psychic companion. Regrets are accompanied by plans to pay back society with good deeds and high moral values.

The correction officers often told me, "Just wait and see, when they get out off comes the religious paraphernalia. They won't continue dancing, reading, studying anything worthwhile; they're going back to the thug life. You're wasting your time."

I have come to see a grain of truth in these warnings. For a few men Facebook becomes a dangerous and exhilarating place. After decades of isolation, within minutes they can reconnect with dozens of people from their past. Many men are emotionally the same age as when they were locked up, without the confidence and experience to present a grown man's persona, and unflattering Facebook identities are created. The temptation is to be seen as cool and tough. This is seductive since there are still many restrictions placed on travel and curfews, but on Facebook one can travel anywhere at any time.

They "friend" me—I accept. The profile pictures are the first clue to how they want to present to the larger society; a man in a three-piece suit smiling in the sculpture garden of the Museum of Modern Art, to half-nude pictures, eyes glazed over as if in a drug stupor, and every-thing in between. One man, posted pictures showing women in compromising sexual situations, men with their backs all scratched up as if they had just had rough sex, videos making fun of overweight women, handicapped people, animals copulating, giving the impression women are good for only three things, cooking, cleaning, and sex. Five women contacted me and complained about one man's postings, since they used my better judgment in deciding to accept his friend request in the first place. Subsequently, some "unfriended" him, and all blocked his posts. One parent from FiguresInFlight 4 questioned my judgment in including this man in the *Welcome to the World* project. When confronted he was defensive. Our relationship ended.

When we received the letter from "Miss Stanford," all of the men were recently released. Although I stand by my decision to include them in *Welcome to the World*, if we had to mount the piece years after they were freed, the decision might be different. Over time their lives change. At that time their behavior was impeccable. Out of the six, I have lost touch with three, so I have no information about them. The pictures I find offensive on Facebook might be acceptable in their culture but not in mine. Cultural differences appear, creating obstacles to understanding. Differences that don't exist in prison seep back in and create new divisions.

The years in prison take a terrible toll on them. After all the introspection and admitting of wrongdoing that occurs in prison, and the fear outside coping with just crossing a busy street, they are not as open to criticism when free. Many suffer from traumatic childhoods, followed by long incarcerations, coming out with post-traumatic stress disorders.

Looking at my own life, I saw that all of my "sins" could be explained by events in my life not in my control. My philosophy teacher said there is no such thing as free will; all of us are too asleep, and unconscious to be responsible for our actions. Nevertheless, free will, even if it is only an unrealistic utopian ideal, must be aspired to or we are doomed to even more chaos in this world.

Chapter 19

————— ❦ —————

Flight Changes

I often leave the kitchen cabinet doors open, no matter how many times Sam has hit his head in the past forty-eight years. It takes too long. I am hyper inside, all the time, filled with nervous, near-hysterical energy. Unless I am sick, I rush from one thing to another, making careless mistakes. Dancers in FiguresInFlight have asked me over and over to label CDs properly. The poor kids have to go through every CD looking for the song we need to rehearse. But labeling is meticulous, boring sit-down work. I leave it up to the students to search for the music.

Always in a hurry, I left a homemade DVD that I'd stuck in a CD case labeled *Lester Horton Technique in* the lobby of the prison after dance class. An officer found it, looked inside, saw it was incorrectly labeled and assumed I might be sneaking in contraband films. What could those be? Pornography? Instructions on how to escape? I was in trouble.

I was initially informed that this offense could be cause to terminate my volunteer status. Then my transgression was down-graded. All I was required to do was be reoriented, refreshed on the rules, procedures, and shown a thirty-five-minute infomercial about the "games inmates play," their criminal minds, and the cunning ways they groom volunteers to break the rules. Already rebellious, I braced myself for an onslaught of propaganda.

But the administrator who reoriented me was kind, patient, and caring. Remembering my bravado, the pride I took in breaking the rules, brought me up short and had me searching my soul. Dehumanizing though they may be, the rules also exist to protect both prisoners and volunteers.

RULE 1 - No touching.

Gently pushing a dancer's back closer to the floor to increase flexibility is one thing with a teenager, another with a grown man who's been deprived. In thousands of instances, I have no way to be sure what might have been misconstrued. I never considered what pain my gentle feminine touch might awaken.

RULE 2 - Don't give them any personal information.

I assumed that I was breaking this rule every time I used an example from my own life in teaching philosophy. Wrong. The rule applies to phone numbers and home addresses. The administrator did say that this rule is somewhat obsolete in the internet era, when anyone can find anyone in minutes. "But that's no reason to disobey," she said.

RULE 3 - Don't do any favors for them. Don't bring anything they give you out of the prison.

When a volunteer does a special favor, such as getting a prisoner a lawyer, calling a family member, or bringing in information from the internet, it opens the door to the possibility of more, including the possibility of bringing in information that could be used negatively. In the reorientation film a story was told about a man who beseeched an officer to get a letter to his wife. The officer obliged since the prisoner was in tears, begging for information about his children. When the man got out, he went straight to the address the officer provided and murdered his wife. This is exceptional but good reason for caution.

The men are needy. The volunteers are kind. Better to draw a clear bright line on the side of safety.

Between five and fifteen of the eight hundred men in Woodbourne are in my program at any given time. They're the top tier, mostly college educated, already in the process of recreating themselves as better men, willing to risk ridicule and devote time and effort to dance. Not one has ever asked me to do anything untoward.

RULE 4 - Don't talk or write about the men in public. Well, it's a bit late for this one. If you are reading this, there are three possibilities: I've been tossed out, have no more interested students, or have somehow gained the support of the New York State Department of Corrections in changing the rule.

The rules are a double-edged sword. You can read them, as I did at first, as an arbitrary, bullying document meant to dehumanize. Or you can consider that they are the Department of Corrections' best effort at protecting both prisoners and volunteers from temptations, compli-cations, and invasions of privacy.

Before reorientation, I'd thought that once a man was released the rules no longer applied. To my alarm, I've been told that no contact is allowed outside the context of a preapproved reentry program. It's a little late to fix this one. Dozens of YouTube videos, Facebook pictures, Indrani's documentary and much more are clear, troubling evidence. After reorientation, I made an attempt to delete what I could. If you Google "Susan Slotnick prison" you get hundreds of hits. My only hope is that no one will take the trouble to try to end my personal re-entry program of breakfast at my house. I don't remember how the tradition began, whose idea it was, but twelve men have left the prison on a Tuesday at 9 AM and arrived at 9:45 to take their first walk of freedom up my driveway. Because they've had decades of bad food, I set a table with beautiful dishes and cutlery. The menu: fresh salad, fruits, bagels, rolls, cheese platter, omelets, sweets, coffee and juices.

The more I appreciated the administrator's sincerity the worse I felt. I'm not used to being dishonest. Honesty is a privilege I'd long taken for granted, the result of being my own boss and not dependent on a bureaucracy for my survival.

For a heartbeat or two I considered changing my plans for the following Monday. Felix Conception was coming home after twenty-eight years. He'd arranged a ride straight to my house for breakfast. It was all planned. In his last Sunday dance class, Felix had been so hyper we could almost see sparks flying from him. I told him to calm down for his own sake. "I can't!" he said.

Now I was signing my name to a paper saying that I understood that I was forbidden to have any contact with him on the outside. It had been twenty-eight years since Felix ate at someone's home. For the last two of those years, he was a dancer. I did get video of Felix bounding up my driveway for a hug, but I didn't put it on YouTube.

In addition to the usual menu, Felix asked for chocolate croissants. Inside, Felix had been intense. His normal state was hyper and energetic; once in a while he'd get miserably low and depressed, but he would pull himself out of it by the next class. At the breakfast table sat a calm and centered man, comfortable in his own skin. At ease, at last. He was flanked by his two poised nephews, both young men well-dressed, educated, and happy to have their uncle back. To cancel that breakfast gathering would have felt like a violation of an even more important rule. It's that rule that should bind us all, COs and prisoners and volunteers, teachers and students. Scrooge learned it in a dream. Lots of people learn it the hard way. It's been called the golden rule.

We had a wonderful time. Felix could not stay for too long; he had to report to his parole officer. But before he left, we danced a salsa, a shared moment of newborn freedom without all the restrictions, then he left promising, "I will not be like the others, I will stay in touch with you". He called me three times. Over time the calls became fewer, but he kept his word and has stayed in touch.

Move into the world, my friend Felix. Put prison behind you. Someday I will do the same.

Epilogue

<hr/>

Forever Mystery

After fifteen years of every Sunday with the prisoners, they still remain a mystery. Day one in the boy's prison to yesterday in the men's prison, I will never know their experience. The more I am in prison the less I know and understand. These men, my friends, are such sweet people, yet at some moment early in their lives they might have raped, murdered and robbed.

Maimonides said, "Teach thy tongue to say 'I do not know', and thou shall progress."

There is so much I do not know. I don't know how much good I've done. I will never know what will stick with them when they face the perils of life as free men. But I accept what Maimonides said, not knowing is progress.

I will only see a small fraction of what will result from all the time, love, and attention I have given to my students in and out of prison. Each one will disseminate the gift of dance and philosophy through their own lives, in their own way. One man, deported to Haiti after his release, told me he is teaching the dances to the street children in Port-au-Prince. Andre is teaching young people recovering from heroin addiction. Bethany will continue to teach dance in prison way after my life is over. Many of the young people who danced in FiguresInFlight are interested in careers related to social justice. A former Woodbourne inmate, currently an NYU PhD candidate wants to interview me for his thesis. A student at the University of Mississippi read an article in

Dance Teacher Magazine and contacted me asking how she can start teaching dance in a prison near her hometown.

When I began there was only one dance program in a men's prison. Maybe fifty years from now dance in prison will be commonplace.

I have tossed seeds into a wild untended garden. Many conditions, not within my control, water, sun, soil, and temperature, determine if a seed becomes a flower. I can only hope for many flowers, trust in the elements and have the humility to accept the outcome.

When I began this memoir, I tried to find Rivera, Dudley, and some of the other boys from Highland Correctional Facility. Twenty years have passed. What did they remember? What was their take away, years later, from the time we shared? I wanted to include that in this writing. I could not find anyone. Their names were too commonplace.

I sent a message over Facebook to a young man with an unusual name: "I am looking for someone with your name who I taught dance to years ago in Highland? Could that be you?"

Two years later, on a night when I was heartbroken trying to make sense of the misogynistic posts, and the end of the relationship with the man who posted them, I received this message:

> Omg yes! I think about you all the time! How are you! I'm sorry I never got your message dear; it was filtered out for some reason. I just randomly went through my contacts, found it, two years later! And thank god I did. I think about you a few times every week of my life. Something always brings back this crazy nostalgia from all you taught me that I hold so close to my heart as every bit of who I am today.
>
> I want you to know that I respect you for all you have done in the time we spent with each other. I grew and learned and became a better stronger person because of you. I can honestly say you saved my life, a few times. I had wanted to commit suicide

and with what you enlightened me to in prison I found a way to keep my head up above water; keep myself from drowning.

Thank you thank you thank you a million times.

And what's that song, the stardust song we danced to?

The song was "Woodstock." I wondered why that song, of the hundreds I played for them, captured his interest after so many years? Could it be this lyric?

We are stardust, we are golden
We are billion-year-old carbon
and we got to get ourselves back to the garden!

The path back is strewn with wounds and unfathomable joys. I carry with me my mother and father, Ahmed the shoe-shine boy, each of the thousands of students in and out of prison, and every disappointment, loss, and heartbreak I have endured. I have painted many pictures, and made hundreds of dances. My husband Sam, the thirteen-year-old boy my mother picked for me, is now in his seventies. We have celebrated our forty-seventh anniversary as I write this.

We are stardust, as old as time, and forever young, full of mystery and continuance.

Afterword

Although it took several years, it felt as if I had lost my prison program, all chances to create choreography, attention residencies, and the FiguresInFlight dance companies overnight. There were days when the emptiness, hour after hour, was like quiet panic in the center of my heart. I asked myself, "Who am I without all of that?"

No answer. But I stuck with the question.

I remembered meeting Joy Dillingham at the fasting resort. She said something that I remembered for forty years, words which seemed inconsequential at the time. I had an inkling it would mean something important someday.

Dr. Gross, who ran the resort, was an expert on fasting and natural hygiene. He could talk for hours offering concrete facts from memory. Miss Dillingham offhandedly said, "I have to bring someone up from the School of Practical Philosophy to unburden Dr. Gross from his knowledge, since he is aging."

That's me, now. I have accrued so much wisdom, developed my talents over half a century for painting, writing, teaching and making dances with no outlet in sight for dispersing any of it. It was a burden that hung heavy like a wet winter coat worn in hot weather until last night.

For two years, I tried to get back into the prison. The prison break in 2015 at Clinton Correctional Facility caused massive panic in New York prisons. The bureaucracy thickened to a hard implacable dissenting compound. Hyper-caution about new programs and fear that civilians would make grave judgment mistakes made it easier to say "no" than work through the obstacles, until last night.

I tried to get back inside, sponsored by Rehabilitation Through the Arts, as an art teacher rather than a dance teacher. I also wrote proposals for teaching a straight philosophy class based on the Gurdjieff concepts. I tried to forge an inroad to improve the lives of immigrant children, joined a committee to help refugees, and continued to knock on the door of prison organizations. None of it resulted in utilizing my potential, until last night.

Network's mission is to create caring communities comprised of men and women who come together voluntarily in maximum- and medium-security New York State prisons for the purpose of learning to live together, trust one another, help one another and rebuild their lives. They opened their arms and let me in last night.

In the same room at Woodbourne Correctional Facility, where I spent 14 years, 720 weeks, three hours a week, over 2,000 hours, I began an endeavor which turned out to be the most rewarding three hours of all the time I spent in that room.

Thirty-five men in state greens, a different population than in the dance program, more diverse and some "long-timers," elderly, who would never have volunteered to dance, entered and took a seat in an oblong configuration of pre-set chairs.

I was there to teach attention, consciousness and presence. On my own, I am not good at paying attention and remembering to be present. When I teach these concepts a state of grace envelops me and at least for those few hours I embody the practice fully to my and the students' advantage. The teachings I learned from Frank Crocitto thirty-five years earlier come back to me, since I was blessed with my father's memory; it was only put to a different use this time than remembering numbers.

Only 10 miles from Woodbourne Correctional is the Monticello Casino and Raceway. Playing slot machines is a guilty pleasure which enables me to reach a pinnacle of inattention, unconsciousness and escape from present reality. Last night, before going inside, I spent several hours playing my favorite slot machine, "Great Africa," strange preparation for a philosophy class based on "waking up," but it renewed my energy and focus like a mid-afternoon snooze.

Then, in the long corridor room in the belly of the prison, magic happened. I have always had magical experiences, what the saints and spiritualists would call happenings in another realm of reality, and coincidences beyond chance. This book did not include those moments because language used in ordinary life is inadequate to describe the indescribable. Trying merely downgrades and trivializes such occurrences.

When I joined the Gurdjieff group led by Frank Crocitto 35 years ago, I met a beautiful young woman named Emily Boardman. We became friends. Eventually, we each left the group filled with passion to make the world a better place. In Judaic tradition we are commanded to "heal the world." I can't remember a time when that was not my greatest wish. Emily started an AIDS retreat and hospice. She was present and helpful to dying men and women in her care. After that she became a minister and a Quaker.

The men went around the room saying their names and how they were feeling: tired, optimistic, wanting to be free, and excited were some of the responses. An older grey-haired gentleman said that he wished the pain in his sciatic nerve would go away.

The class went well, an understatement since any other description would be lofty to the extreme of absurd extravagance.

I hope I am up to the task of writing about what happened next.

With ten minutes left, I asked if the men had any comments or questions for me. I was expecting questions about the material covered in the session. The elderly man with the pain in his hip raised his hand to half-mast.

I have never had the hair really stand-up on my arms. That always seemed a figure of speech, not a physical case of the chills. But when he asked, "Do you know someone named Emily Boardman?" I was stupefied.

Regaining my composure I asked, "How do you know her?"

"I have been in prison for 55 years. I am a lifer. She comes to visit me. What's your name? I will call her tonight. You sound exactly like her."

There is no way I sound like her. She has a New England high-brow accent. Even if she said the word, "fuck," she would sound high class. I, on the other hand, never quite recovered from learning to speak during my first five years in the borough of Brooklyn, New York. If we sounded alike, it wasn't our voices but our intentions and expressions from the years in the Gurdjieff group we spent together.

In the morning I called Emily who responded with laughter, but not because it was humorous. The sound was sheer delight, joy, and merriment. The gentleman had not been able to reach her the night before, since making a phone call from prison is an ordeal.

This is what she told me. "He committed only one crime. Thousands of men get long sentences who have worse crimes and are paroled, but the family, most already dead, wrote letters to keep him inside, and now descendants of his victim write dozens of letters each time his case comes up for review. He is brilliant, a very special person also an extremely gifted artist. I have been so worried about him. I need to be in Massachusetts for the next several months and cannot visit. He was very depressed when I saw him last week because I cannot see him in the foreseeable future. You have no idea what this means to him. You were sent. It's a mystery."

I also called my dear friend, former deputy of programming Jean King, who in spite of her modesty is in a large part responsible for all I have accomplished inside prison walls. She told me to call the director of Network and tell him what happened. At first I was reluctant since I don't know him very well. The story might fall on his ears as, God forbid, the hocus-pocus ramblings of an aging hippie.

I recovered the piece of paper on which I had scribbled his name from the garbage. This is what he said when I reached him: "Oh my God! That man! I know him well. He was in Network in another facility and I was very close with him. One night I went and asked the men where he was; he never missed a meeting. They said he was transferred. Just like that. No goodbyes. I feel like crying. I thought I would never see him again. I will see him again! I am going with you next week. This is a miracle!"

I have no words of explanation, no editorializing on the esoteric meaning of life, just some simple advice to you who are reading this. Stay the course. Heal the world.

If you don't do it, who will?

Susan Slotnick
April 6 2019

Part II: Covid Diary

I wrote these Covid Essays because the local paper closed

Afraid if I had nothing to write my brain would decompose

To coin the masters words who understood so well

From "my heat oppressed brain" came words that do foretell

You can keep your sense of humor and wits about you too.

When pen is put to paper you can have a big breakthrough

You might wonder why here and not in a brand new book.

Truth be told I have spend enough time and money on this here gobbledygook

   -   Susan Slotnick, Summer 2020

Day One: COVID GAMBLING

Shmo (Yiddish) - foolish, stupid, naive

How could I know what was to come the day the drive over the mountain, past acid-green trees with leaves no bigger than house flies, heralded the onset of a springtime of death?

It was a day to be outside, smelling air still tinged with cold but promising the season to come; a season I took for granted would mean new life. Had I known I would be spending the next several months inside, I might have made a better choice than to go to a casino, where nighttime happens during the day. But I wanted to play my favorite slot machine, "Great Africa," where big bold animals found on the

Serengeti Plane burst onto the screen revealing the amount of coins won by serendipity.

I had heard about the virus but did not pay more than a modicum of attention. All I did was take a slightly enhanced precaution, washing my hands every hour or so. Hundreds of people touch the exact place on each machine before their good or bad luck leads them to another game. Intermittently they eat, drink, and go to the bathroom.

Before the catastrophe, I enjoyed being around the type of person gambling at ten AM in a dark environment, where people are props and flashing lights seem alive with promise. Women dressed like cocktail waitresses, cleavage abounding, serve alcohol to old folks, some in wheelchairs. others with walkers.

The gamblers wearing protective masks were predominantly Chinese. They came by the hundreds from New York City on busses to play slots specifically designed for them, like the popular "Voyages of Zheng He."

A woman who sat next to me asked if I was worried about the virus. She told me her 92 year old mother, a diabetic in a wheelchair, was also in the casino, "But she is wearing a mask."

I told her "I heard that only protects from giving it, not getting it."

Six hours later, having thrown away money like a real *shmo*, I drove back over the mountain unaware my gambling days were over, maybe forever.

COVID INTROSPECTION

Mishpachah (Yiddish) - family

Stuck at home with the hubby. I love a challenge. How to shop? What to touch? How close? How far? What will be my guiding star? I will write a poem to pass the time at home:

I met him when I was just eleven.

His name was Sam, only one of seven

Boys who followed me all around

On the night my mother thought I drowned.

I was caught on the beach kissing a boy

My sister was the supposed decoy

She turned out to be a crappy ploy.

I was beat so bad the policeman came

Sam years later my husband became

Now 64 years after he's still around

Locked in together just surround sound.

Enough already! It's getting corny

I search for a snack, feeling forlornly.

Eating while quarantined is magnified in importance to a running reverie, beginning in my mouth, then migrating to my frontal cortex, the boss part that controls important cognitive skills, emotional expression, problem solving, judgment, and sexual behaviors.

My habit: Eating, poo poo, weighing, myself, and then eating, weighing myself, eating, weighing myself again. No sex. More eating, more poo, more stepping on the scale. Some sex.

With no one else to watch, nothing to do, I loom large in my own life, chock full of hyper-self scrutiny. Have I always weighed myself so much?

Who knew, at 13, I was gorgeous, a real budding babe? Since Covid, my high school graduating class (1963) has begun a Facebook page. I received this message from Eugene Guttnawar, a 76 year old junior high school boy: "Hello Suzie Meltzer, I hope you won't take offense. You were the prettiest girl in the school. All the boys stopped just to watch you walk down the hall."

Who knew! I wasn't fat. My mother put me on diet pills once my weight ballooned to 128 pounds: Obetrol, an amphetamine psycho-stimulant, speed. It stimulated my psychosis alright. That was the most optimistic year of my life. That is until 3 AM, when the happy future planning wore off, the insomnia set in, the appetite came back, and I crept in the dark to the kitchen for a snack of peanut butter and matzo.

Every day Mommy weighed me and then weighed herself. We hopefully pooped shortly after, then ate breakfast. Who knew until Covid I was continuing the mommy/daughter ritual 63 years later, still hanging out with old time *mishpachah*, locked in my house as well as in the past.

COVID MARRIAGE

Bashert (Yiddish) - Destined, predestined, fated, meant to be

This is going to be fun, an adventure. My old groom and I never spend hours on end together in our lovely little space. At the beginning, with all the death outside, our love was resuscitated for a short interlude because of the show "Fiddler on the Roof."

We made a video. I stuck a dish towel over my head, propped my Iphone up against the computer and we sang, "Do you love me? Do

I what? Do you love me? Do I love you? With our daughters getting married, and there's trouble in the town, you're upset, you're worn out, go inside, go lie down! Maybe it's indigestion,"… and so on. We sent the video to our daughters.

The least effusive of the three reacted, "This is my favorite thing of all time." A win.

We danced together in the kitchen, sunshine reflected on the floor.

Then the weather changed. It started with the robbery. For ten years I have collected hundred dollar bills, 30 of them, tucked them deep into the crevices of the couch inside a green bank bag. I went for a short social distancing walk around the block and when I came home, the stash was gone like magic. (Magic. I just flashed on Trump saying the virus "would disappear like magic" while he waved his tiny hand in a surprisingly graceful gesture)

I realize now my habit of hiding the money in a spot under a window for a decade could have been observed by a stranger. I took the treasure out of its hiding place often. I counted the wampum every few days whenever I needed to take out a Ben Franklin. My mood went from joyful to miserable.

To pass the time I watched the Amazon Prime documentary about Ted Bundy, "Falling For A Killer." A mood match.

"Suddenly the Ted I knew disappeared. His eyes changed darker. His skin became grey."

Yes, I thought that's what happened after the robbery. A woeful caliginous mist fell on us and my hubby couldn't do anything right. No dancing. No sex. The self-scrutiny ratcheted up to an internal unbearable decibel. How to get unstuck? For the thousandth time, time itself, with tears and talking, after a few days, makes the trouble go away like magic. But anyone married for a long time knows, like a virus, there will be a second wave, recurrences in the fall. Nevertheless, 53 years means it was *Bashert* after all.

COVID FEAR

Der·shrok'·n far (Yiddish) - afraid

This spring, the coldest in my lifetime, prevents walking in woods, where the animals have become brazen since almost all traffic has stopped. Even bears have been sighted on main roads. Yesterday, out the same window through which my stash was seen by the culprit, were eighteen deer of all sizes starring at me as if to say, "Fuck you, human. It's our world now. You ruined it enough already."

Finally, the temperature rose to 57. I was *der·shrok'·n far*, afraid to compete with the creatures, invade their new found turf and go for a stroll. But I did.

"Lions, tigers, and bears! Oh my!" Lines and lyrics enter my head like wind. A song just arrived carried on the air: the 1927 Al Jolson classic, "Me And My Shadow."

I will rewrite:

"Me and my behavior

Sitting all alone in the house.

So much time to savor

How much I love my spouse.

When is it time to eat lunch?

The organic stuff I made.

No, Not time now for brunch,

Toast with marmalade.

Yes it's me and my ole self

Revisiting all that's past.

My life now on the shelf

For as long as this will last.

COVID MEMORIES

I was 14, a bad kid, flunking in school, smoking a pack a day, staying up all night watching TV while the strangers I lived with slept. The school nurse saw a black rash on my neck, took a swab soaked in alcohol, rubbed it across my skin and it turned black. Humiliating. I never washed my face properly. Thick black liquid eyeliner drips trailed down my face for days.

The summer of my 15th year, I escaped all of who I thought I was. I went to Girl Scout camp. In those days there were no dude ranches for incorrigibles. Nevertheless, the camp functioned the same way. The cure was magic. I was a counselor. No boys. No make-up. No parental strangers.

I fell in love with children. The bad seemed to melt like the make-up I wore to cover my true self. I found my home, a pine forest. I had to walk up away from the campgrounds, the laughter and frolicking, and the smell of massive amounts of carbohydrates prepared to stuff into the campers. What words to describe the place; mystical, magical, inscrutable, other-worldly, haunting, mesmerizing, and totally unknowable, just like my 15 year old self.

I feel my 15 year old presence with me now, like an entity from a science fiction film. She's inside me and hovering outside of me. I believe I love her, my 15 year old self, sheltering in place within me.

COVID MOTHER'S DAY

Ma'·meh·leh (Yiddish)-Mother

I always marveled at how much it meant to other women. A friend made a long list and disseminated it to her eleven adult children. She required housework, gardening, carpentry, painting, and tasks as personal as hair dyeing and make-up application. Also flowers with loving poems of appreciation, sappy epistles, like this one:

"My mother, my friend so dear

Throughout my life you're always near.

A tender smile to guide my way

You're the sunshine to light my day

Forever in my heart you'll stay."

I am not automatically a carte blanche fan of mothers, my mother in particular.

I'll call her Sylvia because that was her name. I preferred calling her "Mommy," in the hope that the endearment might begin to feel endearing. "Don't call me Mommy. It's for little children. Address me as 'Mother.'" That was her title. She thought it sounded more high class.

I will call her "Mommy" now because she's dead; still I will not be obedient.

Every Mother's Day I sent her flowers. Every Mother's Day she complained, "Anyone can make a phone call. I don't want flowers. I want you to go to the store, pick out a card, put it in an envelope, address it, put a stamp on it, go to the post office and mail it. I want you to put yourself out." Mother's Day was only one of many circumstances where I was told to, "put myself out."

I couldn't give a card unless I found one with this message:

"Mother, my nemesis who I should fear

Our mother/daughter connection is certainly queer.

Throughout my life you've been so destructive.

All contact with you is so unproductive.

You darken each day with your lousy personality.

As a mother, you are definitely an abnormality."

The card would be decorated with pastel drawings of poison ivy and poison oak wrapped around a black picket fence.

She taught me all I know about being a mother. Like an M.C. Esher lithograph where the positive space and the negative space depict the same image. All I did was the opposite of her in all parenting moments. My method worked.

When my three daughters were upset and sad, I often gave this injunction, "Onward and upward. Be like Barbra Streisand at the end of 'Funny Girl.' She is singing about nothing stopping her, hopeful, powerful and full of herself."

Early the morning of Covid Mother's Day I turned on the computer and there in all their irreverent glory were my three daughters, split screen, lip syncing at the top of their lungs to Barbara's finale from "Funny Girl," "Don't Rain On My Parade!"

During the credits at the end, Bob Dylan sang "Forever Young," a lullaby he wrote for his oldest son. Every night of their childhoods, I placed my hand on my daughters' foreheads and recited the lyrics, a bedtime blessing.

After reciting those lyrics thousands of times, my girls blessed their *ma'·meh·leh* on Covid Mother's Day, "Thank you, to my *ma'·meh·leh*. I couldn't have done it without you."

Best Mother's Day greeting ever.

COVID COLONOSCOPY

Mittendrinen - In the middle of everything else, crazy this had to happen too!

Bissel meshugeh- a little crazy

Oy vey- not good

Kish mir in tuchus- kiss my ass

Mittendrinen, during the aforementioned relationship with my digestive processes and close monitoring of my weight, a letter arrives from the doctor telling me it's time for my colonoscopy.

I haven't left the house in 10 weeks. Nevertheless, I make an appointment for the procedure. I receive ten pages of instructions:

"LOW RESIDUE DIET UNTIL 6PM THE DAY BEFORE YOUR APPOINTMENT."

Who knew I had a suspicious colon? Or was the doc trying to sell an unnecessary procedure at a time when our life savings were leaving nothing more than residue?

" THEN, AFTER 6PM UNTIL MIDNIGHT YOU MAY ONLY HAVE CLEAR LIQUIDS."

I Google "Is vodka a clear liquid?

"Although alcohol is a clear liquid, it can make you dehydrated. You should NOT drink alcohol during the preparation for your test."

The instructions also said, "Drink as much liquid as you can up until midnight."

After waterlogging, why should one harmless glass of vodka be such a threat? I Google, "Can I drink vodka before being anesthetized?"

"Scientists in Germany confirmed alcohol before anesthesia lowers immune system function. Mice who had abdominal surgery after being fed alcohol promptly were infected with a flu–like pneumonia."

Oy vey.

I took a roke of weed. Without going into the horrid happenings inside my descending intestine, the doctor said it failed the residue diet test. They sent me home to try again.

I was confident and better prepared the following week.

"Have you had anything to eat or drink in the last four hours?"

I lied and said one half of a butterscotch LifeSaver at 6:30 AM.

"That is very bad. The residue from the half LifeSaver could lodge in your esophagus and come up while you are unconscious and kill you."

Actually it had been three butterscotch Lifesavers and one ounce of water at 8AM. I didn't tell the anesthesiologist the truth. I wanted it to be over.

"You look terrified! It's okay. Only a speck of a LifeSaver. If it was more, I would not continue the procedure, since you could choke, causing death!"

Propofol. Delicious unconsciousness.

Just as I was going under, a song came on the radio. "Wow!" I said to the nurse.

"Do you want me to change the station?"

I could barely accomplish a weak, "No." The BeeGees' "Stayin' Alive" was just fine to drift off to.

"You don't have cancer."

I coulda *kish mir in tuchus*, but I am not as flexible as I used to be.

COVID POLITICS

Mishegas (Yiddish) - Craziness

I thought it would be charming to be irreverent and whimsical in light of the global affliction, but then I knew his name, George Floyd, and it became offensive of me in my own eyes to joke about this moment on Earth.

Einstein said "No problem will ever be solved by the same consciousness that created it." I am against violence, looting and burning down buildings. Einstein's wisdom circled on a loop with each horrific news item, each new thought. The public consciousness, like a septic system already overflowing with deep troubles about the pandemic, the man whose name I will not say, the fool in the chalky "people's house" who removed millions of human beings' health coverage at a time when sickness and death proliferated from sea to shining sea, was choked anew by the reemergence of one of this nation's ugliest issues.

In 1999, when the World Trade Organization Ministerial Conference was scheduled to take place in Seattle, 40,000 anti-globalization activists showed up to protest the meeting and shut it down. Protestors blocked traffic preventing delegates from getting to the conference. Police responded by firing tear gas, pepper spray and rubber bullets. Storefronts were destroyed. Fires were set in dumpsters, then pushed into intersections. The tires of police cars were slashed. 600 people were arrested. The vandalism caused $20 million in damages. Nothing changed. Globalization continues unchecked.

On the evening of July 13, 1977, New York City went dark. At the precise moment I was working in the sportswear department at Saks Fifth Ave. It occurred to me that I could scoop up an armful of cruise wear, walk out and enjoy a new warm weather wardrobe gratis. I was tempted. Others overcame the inhibition.

The blackout was marred by pervasive arson and looting. When power was restored on July 14, the actions of wild-eyed young men emerging from shattered storefronts with new television sets were all over the news. Over 1,600 stores were damaged. Over 1,000 fires were reported and 3,776 people were arrested. It was the largest mass arrest in New York City history. Without a political motivation, the only incentive was capriciousness and gain. Protests, too, are an apt hiding place for charlatans. That hasn't changed.

The 1965 riots in the Los Angeles neighborhood of Watts were the worst in that city's history. Watts was a low-income community, mostly African-American with high unemployment, poverty and racial discrimination. Its residents were regularly on the receiving end of police brutality. The situation degenerated into widespread violence for six days, at a cost of $40 million and 34 lives. Police brutality didn't stop.

Martin Luther King, Jr. was assassinated on April 4, 1968 a time of great turbulence due to opposition to the Vietnam War, Civil Rights, and the generation gap. Riots occurred in more than 100 major American cities. Chicago saw a full 28 blocks decimated by fires and looting.

Arson was so extensive, many buildings so badly damaged, that they had to be torn down, rendering many hundreds of people homeless and costing more than $10 million in damages. What changed? We still need the clarion call for Black lives to matter.

After the King assassination, I attended a rally comprised of all Black people. When I tried to speak, I was booed. One person screamed, "Get her out of here!" In my naivety I retorted, "Go yell at the White people who didn't show up. Not at me." That was my first encounter with what has since become commonplace: allies criticized for "White fragility," discomfort and defensiveness on the part of a White person when confronted with racial injustice and Black anger.

Since George Floyd was murdered by police, I have participated in a few "White fragility" conversations with only other White people; a whole lot of mishegas.

Let's call them White Persons #1 and #2.

#1, "You are a racist"

#2, "No I am not. I am against looting, which often hurts Black people the most."

#1, "You are so White in your mindset, you don't understand Black rage."

#2, "You understand Black rage? You're White, too."

#1, "No! I am not and never say that to me again. I live in the hood with all Black people."

#2, "That doesn't make you Black."

#1, "I understand where they are coming from, why they loot."

#2, "That's nuts. I am against violence, property damage."

… And here is what we both accomplished for the Black Lives Matter movement: Damaging our friendship.

My daughter is a very militant pointer-outer of other people's racism. I can't really blame her; after all, I raised her with Chaka Wade, my best friend, Dr Margaret Wade-Lewis's child. We co-parented the children all though their young years, three nights a week they had sleepovers. From 1 to 5 years old, they thought they were siblings. I enrolled Rebekah in a Black Nationalist nursery school so she and Chaka could stay together.

Margaret was an anti-Semite, or at the least had anti-Semitic inclinations. She brought Louis Farrakhan to speak at New Paltz College and stood by while he went on an uninterrupted rant about the inherent evil of Jews. A much-loved professor from the Jewish Studies Department was verbally attacked by the Black students while Margaret stood by, allowing the lack of civility, leaving the professor in tears.

In my desire to create empathy and understanding between us, I showed her a gripping documentary about the history of the Jews during the Holocaust.

"Six million Jews died. Nine million slaves died," she said.

Me, person #2, "I didn't know it was a competition."

Rebekah says,

"The conundrum of Margaret making anti-semitic choices while still loving and knowing you, identifying you as her 'best friend,' reminds me of a Jewish friend of mine who has anti-Semitic friends. I asked her how she abides it and she says they excuse her, like this: 'Oh, but you're not Jewish like those Jews who control the media and the wealth of the world, who are either Zionists, Communists, or fascists.' So this weird attitude occurs when confronted with actual evidence of how wrong are our sweeping stereotyping prejudice and racist beliefs. We tend to see an individual we like as an exception and so we can adhere to our internalized racist beliefs. 'Oh! Well I know plenty of

Jews/Blacks/Muslims/Asians/etc. who are no good, but you are different.' This is how we've internalized the racist ideology and how we stay stuck in it.

If you pay attention to people, really pay attention to people, look in their eyes, perceive what you see, listen to what they might say or not say, discipline yourself to approach each encounter with an open mind knowing each person is an individual, see each other and be seen, that is the key,

But it's ridiculously idyllic. I mean silly, rose-colored glasses.

But, Mom, I try to do it as much as possible. And when we perceive others' humanity, it's easier to perceive our collective humanity, and thereby undo racism. That's my belief."

Tyrone, a talented dancer from my prison Modern Dance class, loved me and I loved him. We bonded over the process, the choreography, the mindfulness/attention philosophy, which was the cornerstone underneath the art, the foundation which supported the miracle we collectively created.

With my professional youth company, I choreographed a technically demanding ten minute piece to Nina Simone's masterwork, her version of "Sinner Man," an African American traditional spiritual about a sinner attempting to hide from divine justice on Judgment Day. The level of difficulty was way beyond a grown untrained man's ability but they managed to dance most of the original choreography. Tyrone had a featured part.

We had a special bond, both similarly passionate about Martin Luther King. Every Martin Luther King Day I brought into the prison a recording of "The Drum Major Instinct," my favorite MLK speech. During Black History Month, I alsoI read my published column "My Black History."

"I think of you as a sister, not a White person," Tyrone told me.

To him, a supreme compliment.

Although I appreciated where he was coming from, I wanted him to know that "Whites" and, importantly to me, "Jews" are against racism and do not need to be reinvented in a different skin to be loved.

Will the day come when we judge each person "by the content of their character" as Martin Luther King wished for 50 years ago? Is Covid a wake up call? First we must stop the mishegas and keep our eyes on the prize.

COVID INNER INVENTORY

Kishkes (Yiddish): Jewish dish: a beef or fowl intestine stuffed with a mixture of flour, fat, onion, and seasonings, then roasted.

Slang: Something gets you in your kishkes - means you feel it deeply in your gut.

Shpilkes (Yiddish): A state of impatience, agitation, anxiety, or any combination thereof.

How dare I call my friend Margaret anti-Semitic? She put up with me for decades, my good natured mistakes, my moments of ignorance.

How do I know why she didn't stop Farrakhan?

You can never know what people are feeling in their kishkes, what's motivating them at the core. How entitled and narcissistic we can be, attributing meanings through the dense implacable screen of our accumulated opinions and limited life experiences. Margaret was from Oklahoma, "Susie," she would say, "Oklahoma Blacks are very different from southern, city, or Blacks from any other region."

Margaret's father was a minister. Her ten siblings all became professionals, doctors, lawyers, academicians. I only met her parents and siblings once, during Margaret's battle with a cancerous tumor in her tongue. I spent the day with her family waiting for a call to find out if the cancer had metastasized, whether her tongue would be amputated to save her life.

As a professor with a doctorate in linguistics, renowned for going to the "nth degree" for each student, no matter the sacrifice, losing her ability to speak would be a calamity impossible to contemplate.

Oklahoma Blacks, at least in this family, are patient, polite, and unnervingly calm. The surgery was scheduled for 7 AM. No news, 10 AM, 11 AM, 12 noon, 1 PM all crawl by at a mind-bogglingly slow pace. Every 15 minutes or so, I asked her mother if we should call the hospital for results.

"Suzie," her mother would say, "When her husband calls, we will find out. It's in God's hands. God cannot be rushed."

I am a New York Jew. G-d can, yes, be rushed. Generally we don't believe God decides outcomes alone, without our help. But that's New York Jews. New York Jews are different from Israeli Jews, Arizona Jews, Ethiopian Jews.

The *shpilkes* within was so intense I could have lifted a car, Finally, I could not take another moment and I called Sloan-Kettering. Margaret answered the phone. "Hello," she said.

With that word, the shpilkes released out of me like the steam from a pressure cooker.

If her family thought I had a lot of nerve overriding their suggestions, they would not have attributed my actions to White privilege. I loved her. They knew it. Her mom smiled and said, "Well, Suzie, God worked through you, I suppose. "

There are numerous alternative reasons why Margaret may have allowed Farrakhan to speak uninterrupted. She was polite, patient, and unnervingly calm, answering most questions with, "I can't complain," even when she had more than enough reason to. Her love for the Black students, who often felt silenced in their classes, many coming from inferior schools due to institutionalized racism, entering college less prepared without an even playing field, might have prevented her from publically chastising them. I still feel she should have instructed her students to act civilly.

Through the screen of my life experiences, my New York Jewish culture, I will always hold that point of view.

Never in my life, until this Covid season, have words like racist and anti-Semite been volleyed back and forth so hard and fast, reported in the media, giving the false impression that love has left the conversation. Margaret would say, "Suzie, have patience, faith, and hope," which I would have translated into "put a lid on your shpilkes."

COVID CHANGE IN FORTUNE

Gut fortune (Yiddish): good fortune

An old man, old before his time, although how could I know.

He just looked ancient. He hobbled into the room, in pain from sciatica and his 55 years locked up in airless spaces, with minimal good food and health care, bad teeth showing in a wan smile, sparse gray hairs falling on his shoulders. Resignation and abdication were the expressions he wore, a surrender born of hopelessness. He was never getting out, as famous a murderer as the "Son of Sam."

I googled him. Nothing is secret or sacred anymore. The details, slaughterous, sexual, and hideous, digitized permanently out there, transmitted by the click of a fingertip into eternity.

The next time I saw him, I tried to connect him with the picture on line of a good-looking kid, who, in one moment while on drugs, went amuck beyond comprehension. All I saw was a human: my age, as it turned out, without a single cell in his body from 55 years ago when the crime was committed, wheeling himself into a drab room.

During the ten weeks I was his teacher, I learned we had a lot in common. He was an artist, although his work was not like my art with its wild colors, huge abstracts, and oil paintings of effusive dancers. His art reflected his environment, tight pencil drawings, exquisite realistic details requiring time and patience only a person with no place to go could endure.

Through coincidence, happenstance or magic, we had a good friend in common, his pen-pal, a woman I admired for her propensity to perform good deeds. She called me yesterday.

This is what she said happened to my student, her pen-pal.

He said, "Just like that! Shocking! After a lifetime! Such good fortune for me in the midst of so much bad fortune for others.

A correction officer came to my cell, and said, 'Pack up! You're going home! No parole hearing! It's Covid! That's why. Covid, he said, is giving me my life back!' "

His first action as a free man was to go to the exact crossroads where his life took a turn for the worse, literally a street address.

In the 55 years, the place had changed for the better. He saw dozens of large trees where there had been none. He said, "When I was a boy, this place was desolate, ugly, impoverished and crime ridden. If there had been trees, any beauty at all, it all would have been different. Praise be to trees! And now during Covid, when bad news proliferates exponentially, I will plant some. A sign of life's renewal."

COVID CLEAN-UP

Yiddish:

chazerai - garbage, junk, unsubstantial stuff

Goyish - non-Jew

Chachkies - trinkets and collectables, dusty items you would find in an old lady's house.

Alta cocker - old shithead

"chazerai!" It's fun to pronounce this word in Yiddish, especially if your throat is full of sticky phlegm. It's the Z pronounced with a vengeance from the back of the throat which would spread covid several miles, emptying your respiratory equipment in a single sharp, "CHAZZZZZ."

I once tried to teach it to a non-Jewish friend, a goyish person. Her living space was filled with *chazerai,* old shoes, newspapers, clothes on chairs, floor littered with *mucho chachkies.* She was incapable by virtue of her complete lack of a single Ashkenazi gene to say the word. I told her it would help if she said it in context.

"Go out. Knock on the door. Open it. Peruse the room and say in a disgusted voice, "What the hell is all the *chazerai*? All she could muster was, "What the hell is this higher high?"

Since Covid I am determined to decrease my carbon footprint on the planet for one reason: I could die. Not could, will die, and I do not want my three daughters burdened by my *chazerai* and my *chachkies.*

Out from the deep nooks and crannies of the house we have lived in for 51 years emerge *chazerai* we saved for God knows what reasons.

I am an *alta-cocker,* reading a postcard I wrote from camp when I was 8 years old.

"Dear Mommy and Daddy, I made a bull's-eye in archery and I never want to come home."

From my freshman year at Morris Harvey College in West Virginia, "Hello Parents. My marks are OK. I am in love with the only Jewish boy here, but he has absolutely, totally no interest in me. His name is David and he plays jazz trumpet."

Yesterday, during the pandemic, I emailed him and asked if he had absolutely totally no interest in me, when we were in college.

"What are you doing now?" he asked. So I sent him a YouTube video I recorded that morning of myself dancing to the Alcoholic Anonymous Christian Serenity Prayer.

His reply... "And just for the record, I was NOT uninterested (let alone "totally") in you. You were, after all, one wild and crazy, sexy Jew broad. *L'Chaim!* (To life!) Very nice dance moves for an old chick. Today my father would have turned 120. If he'd only taken better care of himself. He made it to 90, imbibing his daily Tel Aviv cocktail, 2 parts prune juice, 1 part each of hot water and lemon. Yummy!" All these years I had saved four letters from David, one from Vietnam. All very funny. I tossed the letters without regret.

I had saved my high school smoking permit signed by my mother: "Susan Meltzer has permission to smoke in the A-1 building courtyard during morning recess." Tossed that, too.

Out of a dirty carton came forth two faded, crumbling white baby shoes, an inscription reading, "Suzie's first shoes," written on the outside of the left foot. Gloomy reminders of the passage of time.

Also. A letter from my mother:

"Dear Sue,

You asked me to write.

What can I say?

Only that I love you more each day.

And hope you love me in your own little way.

May each day bring your hearts desire

And remember everybody hates a liar.

Your Mom."

A brown piece of cardboard, frayed around the edges reveals this information:

Caledonian Hospital

Brooklyn, NY

Name of baby: Girl Meltzer

Birth Weight: 8 pounds 6 oz.

I stuffed the card in the shoes, and said a prayer of gratitude. During Covid, I am one of the lucky ones, still intact. Then I threw both items away.

A thin piece of yellowed paper the size of a post-it fell from an overturned box into my lap.

In small neatly written letters one side says,

"To Susan Meltzer, Please go to see Miss Cooksey tomorrow. Important!" I have no idea who Miss Cooksey was. My tenure with Cooksey had to have been in high school or my first year in college; after that, I was married with a new name.

Why would I save this? And then I turn it over. In my handwriting is written:

"You shall say to them this word;

Let my eyes run down with tears day and night.

And let them not cease, for my dearly beloved people is smitten with a great wound, with a very grievous blow. Yahweh."

This I will not throw out. I will put it on the refrigerator door. Say it everyday until my dearly beloved planet is no longer smitten with a great wound.

COVID BEFORE AND NOW

Kopdreyenish (Yiddish): troubles, suffering

My life was born of my mother's story

That's no surprise, it's always that way

Her life is an allegory

When sickness led my mother astray

Because of the old epidemic

I became all that I am today.

One hundred years later, what is the truth

How to keep this from hurting the youth

Only one picture of my mother survived from her childhood. A pretty, forlorn little girl in a burlap dress, soup bowl hairdo, hanging on the hem of a somber looking woman dressed entirely in black.

A far cry from the inadvertent video I caught of her in 1974 right after her first face-lift. She sailed into the room ignoring everyone else, looked in the mirror and announced (since I have the clip on tape, I can quote her exactly), "At any age, a woman should take pride in her appearance, keep herself groomed and use all methods available to retain her good looks."

Her mother, my grandma Sadie, was ugly as a fairy tale witch with a personality to match. Grandma Sadie did a lot of pacing and wringing her hands. Her face was dotted with various sized blackheads, color-coordinated with her opaque housedresses. She never wore a bra (did bras exist in Poland in 1850?) Her stockings were rolled up and knotted under the knee leading downward to her clodhopper shoes.

Somehow my grandmother snagged a husband and birthed three children; two as ugly as she and one beauty, my mother.

I never met my grandfather. He died in the flu epidemic of 1917, when my mother was 7.

Mother told me the story many times, identifying the event as "the worst moment of my life. "

"My father was the only person who was kind to me, no one else loved me. He had a little storefront in Brooklyn selling household trinkets. The most expensive item in his store were mirrors, which he rarely sold. It was a big event when he sold a mirror. We were very poor like all the other Jewish immigrants. But when he sold a mirror it was the only time I saw anyone in my family smile. While he was dying the deathbed vigil lasted several days, I was banished from the room until the end when we children were brought in to say goodbye and witness the death. I wandered between the adults, pulling on their clothing to get attention. I remember thinking 'Tell him he sold a mirror today and he won't die;'

"No one paid any attention. I was positive that would keep him from dying but no one listened. I could not be heard over the wailing of the grown-ups. I never felt loved again."

The Spanish influenza pandemic struck terror in the hearts of millions as they watched beloved friends and relatives die. The epidemic left a lasting imprint upon the collective memory, but for my mother it was the defining trauma of her life; Her primal Kopdreyenish.

Afterward she developed a narcissistic personality, which begins when a child is no longer loved or provided for, and self-concern, necessary for survival, lodges in the personality like an out-of-control Medusa. It is incurable, affecting all relationships, creating havoc in families.

My mother's psychic injury was handed down to me and became my core wound. Were it not for the pandemic of 1917 I would be a different person in all my ways, both good and bad.

How many wounds and blessings will meander through the generations from the pandemic of 2020?

As we live in this world dystopian

With all our childhood demons intact

Believe in a future utopian

Your good heart now is packed

With fear and sadness, which overflows

Breaking at the seams of love's deepest core

This will be a time when kindness grows

Because when a heart breaks know for sure

Love and compassion spill out everywhere

So embrace your brokenness with grace

Don't stop or welcome this time of despair.

Just love this broken flawed human race.

That's my story and I am sticking to it.

Susan Slotnick July 21, 2020

Made in the USA
Middletown, DE
19 October 2020